The Handpicked Ninja Foodi Cookbook UK

The Latest Ninja Foodi Recipes Will Help You Get Started with Pressure Cooking, Slow Cook, Steam, Sauté, Dehydrate, and More

Mellie Bradley

© Copyright 2023 – All Rights Reserved

This document is geared towards providing exact and reliable information with regards to the topic and issue covered. The publication is sold with the idea that the publisher is not required to render accounting, officially permitted, or otherwise, qualified services. If advice is necessary, legal, or professional, a practiced individual in the profession should be ordered. -From a Declaration of Principles which was accepted and approved equally by a Committee of the American Bar Association and a Committee of Publishers and Associations. In no way is it legal to reproduce, duplicate, or transmit any part of this document in either electronic means or in printed format. Recording of this publication is strictly prohibited and any storage of this document is not allowed unless with written permission from the publisher.

All rights reserved. The information provided herein is stated to be truthful and consistent, in that any liability, in terms of inattention or otherwise, by any usage or abuse of any policies, processes, or directions contained within is the solitary and utter responsibility of the recipient reader.

Under no circumstances will any legal responsibility or blame be held against the publisher for any reparation, damages, or monetary loss due to the information herein, either directly or indirectly. Respective authors own all copyrights not held by the publisher.

The information herein is offered for informational purposes solely, and is universal as so. The presentation of the information is without contract or any type of guarantee assurance. The trademarks that are used are without any consent, and the publication of the trademark is without permission or backing by the trademark owner.

All trademarks and brands within this book are for clarifying purposes only and are the owned by the owners themselves, not affiliated with this document.

Table of Contents

1 Introduction

2 Fundamentals of Ninja Foodi Max Multi-Cooker

15 4-Week Meal Plan

17 Chapter 1 Breakfast Recipes

Chocolate Banana Bread	17	Spicy Pork Chorizo with Mexican Eggs	22
Cheese Sausage and Egg Strata	18	Tasty Courgette & Cheese Drop Biscuits	23
Banana-Walnuts Oatmeal	18	Israeli Couscous and Veggie	23
Banana-Nutella Stuffed French Toast	19	Rosemary Apricot Scones	24
Breakfast Farro with Apricots	19	Mushroom Congee Breakfast Bowl	24
Steel-Cut Oats with Dried Apples	20	Garlic Cheese Bread	25
Creamy Polenta	20	Jalapeño-Cheddar Bagel Egg Casserole	25
Quinoa Chili with Feta cheese	21	Homemade Gingerbread French Toast Casserole	26
Buckwheat Banana Porridge	21		
Honey Veggie Corn Muffins	22	Creamy Strawberry Oats	26

27 Chapter 2 Soup, Chili and Stew Recipes

French Onion Cheese Soup	27	Creamy Cheese Tomato Basil-Soup	32
Salmon, Leek, and Potato Soup	28	Chili Beef Hot Dog Soup	32
Corned Beef and Beans Chili	28	Pearled Barley-Lentil Soup with Spinach	33
Thai-Style Butternut Bisque	29	Spicy Black Bean Soup	33
Creamy Cheese Chicken Soup	29	Thai Spiced Lentil and Coconut Milk Soup	34
Beef and Sausage Soup with Pepperoni	30	Pepperoni, Cheese Ravioli and Mushroom Pizza Stew	34
Beans and Kale Soup	30		
Cheddar Broccoli and Potato Soup	31	Beef Brisket & Butternut Squash Chili	35
Spiced Yellow Lentil and Spinach Soup	31	Cumin Bacon and Black Bean Chili	36

Yellow Lentil Soup 36	Beef and Mushroom Stroganoff Soup ... 39
Spiced Red Lentil and Pumpkin Soup ... 37	Black-Eyed Peas and Ham Soup 39
Loaded Vegetable and Green Lentil Stew 37	Cheesy Broccoli, Carrot and Cauliflower
Lamb and Carrot Stew 38	Soup 40
Sweet Potato Lentil Soup with Spinach 38	Herbed Kidney Bean and Sausage Soup 40

41　Chapter 3 Vegetable and Sides Recipes

Simple Corn on the Cob (Four Ways) ... 41	Kale and Edamame Salad with Sesame
White Rice with Peas and Swiss	Ginger Dressing 46
Chard 42	Spiced Corn with Jalapeno-Peppers 47
Spanish Rice with Pepper s 42	Jalapeno & Cotija Cheese Potato Pie ... 47
Cheesy Tortellini Alfredo and Peas 43	Cheese Broccoli Potato Cake 48
Cheese Pasta with Broccoli 43	Black Bean and Rice–Stuffed Peppers ... 48
Lemony Mushroom and Leeks Risotto 44	Cheesy Alfredo Pasta with Carrots &
Indian-Spiced Basmati Rice with Peas ... 44	Broccoli 49
Mustard Potato and Bacon Salad 45	Black Bean & Brown Rice Casserole ... 49
Lima Beans with Bacon & Tomato 45	Vegetarian Gumbo with Rice 50
Cheesy Spaghetti with Sausage and	Rosemary Navy Beans..................... 50
Broccolini 46	Autumn Potatoes Egg Salad 51

52　Chapter 4 Poultry Mains Recipes

Greek Chicken and Mixed Greens Salad 52	Cranberry Hot Chicken Wings............ 55
Teriyaki Chicken Wings 53	Turkey Verde and Brown Rice 55
Cajun Chicken and Rice Bowls 53	Lemony Chicken with Artichoke
Tasty Barbecue Chicken–Stuffed Sweet	Avocado 56
Potatoes 54	Cheese and Courgette Stuffed
Indian Curried Chicken 54	Chicken 56

Juicy Chicken Sliders 57	French Onion Cheese Chicken............ 60
Smoked Paprika Turkey Lunchmeat ... 57	Chicken & Dumplings Soup 61
Chicken and Bacon Sandwiches 58	Creamy Curry Chicken Bites 62
Cumin Salsa Verde Chicken............... 58	Marsala Wine Braised Chicken and
Spiced Mango-Chipotle Shredded	Mushroom 63
Chicken 59	Chinese-Style Chicken & Broccoli 64
Balsamic Mozzarella Chicken Veggie	Turkey Meatball and Kale Soup
Salad 59	with White Beans........................... 65

66 Chapter 5 Seafood Mains Recipes

Rice Pilaf withCorn and Prawns 66	Rice Vermicelli 70
Jollof Rice With Prawns & Peas 67	Lemny Salmon with Horseradish Sauce 71
Garlicky Salmon 68	Herbed Clams 71
Delicious Prawns Stew with White	Seafood and Veggie Stew................. 72
Beans & Spinach 68	Herbed Crab Cake 73
Lime Prawns & Corn Salad 69	Prawns and Potatoes with Cocktail Sauce 74
Creamy Seafood and Noodles Casserole 70	Garlicky Buttery Prawns 74
Curried Prawns with Vegetables &	Creamy Seafood Chowder 75

76 Chapter 6 Beef, Pork and Lamb Recipes

Beef and Carrot Stew with Bacon 76	Herbed Beef & Cheddar Croissants 81
Homemade Beef & Beets Borscht 77	Easy Beef and Broccoli 82
Beef Sandwiches with Cheese Sauce ... 78	Pulled Beef with Pappardelle 83
Pulled Pork and Pineapple Sandwiches 78	Red Wine–Braised Beef Short Ribs 84
Beef Lettuce Wraps 79	Garlicky Pork Roast with Red Cabbage 85
Lemony Beef Risotto 79	Beer-Braised Pork with Sauerkraut 85
Coffee-Rubbed Steak and Rice Bowls ... 80	Pulled Lamb Shoulder with Pomegranate &
Korean Beef Rolls 80	Honey Sauce 86

Table of Contents | 03

Pork Chops with Creamy Mushroom Gravy 87	Tasty Pickled Pulled Pork 88
Barbecue Beef & Pasta Casserole 87	Beer-Braised Pulled Beef.................. 89
Beef, Barley and Celery Soup 88	Teriyaki Pulled Lamb 90

91 — Chapter 7 Dessert Recipes

Vanilla Cheesecake 91	Red Wine-Braised Apples 95
Homemade Molten Mocha Cake 92	Best Key Lime Pie 96
Cheesecake with Peaches................. 92	Lemony Tapioca Pudding 96
Classic Cheesecake 93	Vanilla Lemon Cheesecake 97
Delicious Stuffed Peaches 93	Cranberry & Walnuts Stuffed Apples ... 97
Peach-Berry Cobbler 94	Easy White Chocolate Pots De Crème ... 98
Chocolate-Berry Mug Cake 94	Carrot Coconut Cake with Pecans 98
Caramel Brownie Pudding 95	Delicious Maple Crème Brule 99

100 — Conclusion

101 — Appendix Recipes Index

04 | Table of Contents

Introduction

When you want home-cooked meals but are too lazy to make them yourself, the Ninja Foodi Max is an excellent purchase. It has 10 cooking capabilities built into its simple-to-use body, allowing you to roast, bake, grill, make crisp meals, and more, all while saving you time and energy. In reality, the Ninja Foodi MAX Multi-Cooker, as its full name suggests, can air fry food with up to 75% less fat than conventional techniques and pressure cook food up to 70% faster than conventional methods. Due to its enormous capacity, it is a fantastic choice for large families, but you will need enough countertop space or storage space to keep it. However, the curved body's black and stainless steel realization is fashionable. All the cooking settings are available on board in an easy-to-use digital display that may be operated with a single button click. With options like pressure cooking, steaming, grilling, air crisping without oil, baking, roasting, and dehydrating, your standard built-in oven may appear quite obsolete. In addition to a cook and crisp basket, there is a two-tier reversible rack for cooking main dishes and sides at the same time. This is useful for stacking veggies with meats, poultry, or fish. It has TenderCrisp Technology, which crisps food after cooking for an actual oven-cooked flavor. It's simple to throw ingredients into the Ninja and let it do its thing until it's time to eat. Use it to conjure up mouthwatering curries from Friday night fantasies or Sunday roasts that will solidify your position as the family cook to beat.

Fundamentals of Ninja Foodi Max Multi-Cooker

What is Ninja Foodi Max Multi-Cooker?

The old-fashioned iron devices with industrial-looking clamps on the side to prevent the lid from blowing off when the pressure grew too high and a steam valve on top that looked like a train whistle is not what we mean when we say "pressure cooker." We're referring to the slick, fashionable, and multipurpose digital appliances that are transforming kitchen cooking. Ninja Foodi Max is the best option here. This gadget is worth keeping on hand if you need dinner quickly because it can pressure cook 70% faster than conventional versions and can even prepare food from frozen. Without ever taking a cooking lesson, you can quickly and easily make wholesome family dinners with the Ninja Foodi MAX Multi-Cooker. Although having a large capacity is great from a family standpoint, many multi-cookers take a very long time to cook everything since they lack the raw power of a conventional oven. With the NINJA Foodi MAX Multi-Cooker, however, you can cook meals up to 70% quicker than with conventional appliances while still getting succulent, fall-off-the-bone meat thanks to the pressure cook mode. This monster can cook a 3-kilogram chicken in less than an hour, which should satisfy even the hungriest, anxious family members.

Functions

Functions: From juicy steaks and delicately pulled pork to flavorful curries and flawlessly cooked pasta, pressure cooker meals are quick and delectable. Pressure cooking employs very hot steam to seal in liquids and may cook food up to 70% quicker than conventional methods.

1. STEAM:

When cooking delicate items at a high temperature, use steam. Healthy vegetable meals, tender asparagus, and elegant sea bass may all be steamed.

2. SLOW COOK:

Cook your meal more slowly and at

a lower temperature. Slow Warming casseroles, zesty risottos, and filling hotpots may all be prepared up to 12 hours ahead of time so that your supper is ready when you arrive home.

3. YOGURT:
Pasteurize milk and ferment it to make rich homemade yogurt.

4. SEAR/SAUTÉ:
Use the appliance as a cooktop to brown meats, sauté veggies, simmer sauces, and more.

5. AIR CRISP:
With up to 75% less fat than conventional frying techniques, Air Crisp may also be used as an air fryer to prepare meals and sides that require little to no oil, such as crispy fish fingers and chicken wings, and golden chips.

6. BAKE/ROAST:
For tender meats, baked goods, and other items, use the appliance as an oven. Roast succulent nut roasts, hearty vegetable medleys from the Mediterranean, and comforting winter vegetables. Make delicious treats, fresh bread, and cakes that you can be proud of.

7. GRILL:
Grill excellent burgers, salmon fillets, and a crispy topping for mac & cheese.

8. DEHYDRATE:
Dehydrate fruits, vegetables, and meats for wholesome snacking. To make nutritious dried fruit, such as mango, apple, strawberry, and bananas, as well as handmade root vegetable crisps, beef jerky, and dry herbs, dehydrate fresh ingredients.

9. KEEP WARM:
The appliance will automatically switch to the Keep Warm mode and begin

Fundamentals of Ninja Foodi Max Multi-Cooker | 3

counting up after pressure cooking, steaming, or slow cooking. Keep Warm will stay on for 12 hours, or you may press KEEP WARM to turn it off. Keep Warm mode is not intended to warm food from a cold state but to keep it warm at a food-safe temperature.

Step by Step Using It

Air Crisp

1. Either put the Cook & Crisp Basket in the pot or the reversible rack. The basket should have a diffuser attached.
2. Add ingredients to the reversible rack or Cook & Crisp Basket. Put the lid on.
3. To choose AIR CRISP, spin the START/STOP dial after pressing FUNCTION. It will show the current temperature setting. To select a temperature between 150°C and 200°C, press TEMP and then spin the dial.
4. To change the cooking time in minute

intervals up to an hour, press TIME and then spin the START/STOP dial. Simply add 5 minutes to the cooking time to preheat your appliance. To start or stop cooking, press START/STOP.

5. If necessary, you may pull out the basket and open the lid while the food is cooking to shake or toss the contents for more equal browning. Close the cover after lowering the basket back into the pot. Once the lid is shut, cooking will automatically begin again.
6. The appliance will beep and show DONE when the cooking time is over.

Grill

1. Either follow the instructions in your recipe or place the reversible rack in the pot in the upper grill position.
2. After arranging the items on the rack, secure the cover.
3. To choose GRILL, spin the START/STOP dial after pressing FUNCTION.
4. To change the cooking time in minute increments up to 30 minutes, press

TIME and then turn the dial.
5. To start or stop cooking, press START/STOP.
6. The appliance will beep and show DONE when the cooking time is over.

Bake/Roast

1. Fill the pot with the necessary materials and equipment. Put the lid on.
2. Select BAKE/ROAST by turning the START/STOP dial after pressing FUNCTION. It will show the current temperature setting. To choose a temperature between 120°C and 200°C, press TEMP and then spin the dial.
3. To change the cooking time, press TIME, then crank the START/STOP dial in minute increments up to 1 hour, then in 5-minute increments from 1 hour to 4 hours. To start or stop cooking, press START/STOP.
4. The appliance will beep and show DONE when the cooking time is over.

Dehydrate

1. A layer of ingredients should be placed on the bottom position of the two-tier reversible rack in the pot.
2. Place the top layer over the reversible rack as shown below, holding it in place with its grips. After that, add an ingredient layer to the top tier and secure the lid.
3. Select DEHYDRATE by turning the START/STOP dial after pressing FUNCTION. It will show the current temperature setting. To select a temperature between 40°C and 90°C, press TEMP and then spin the dial.
4. Press TIME, then spin the dial to change the cooking time up to 12 hours in 15-minute intervals.
5. To start the dehydration process, close the lid and press START/STOP.
6. The appliance will beep and show DONE when the cooking time is over.

Pressure Cook

1. Place the pot in the cooker base and add 750ml of room-temperature water to the pot.
2. By lining up the arrow on the front of the lid with the arrow on the front of the cooker base, you can assemble the pressure lid. When the lid latches into place, spin it clockwise.
3. A pressure release valve should be in the SEAL position.
4. Press FUNCTION, then choose PRESSURE by using the START/STOP dial. High (HI) pressure and a 2-minute time setting are the default

Fundamentals of Ninja Foodi Max Multi-Cooker | 5

settings for the device. To start, press START/STOP.

5. The display's PRE and some steam leakage suggest there is increasing pressure. The countdown will start once the pressure is at its maximum.

6. The device will beep and show DONE after the countdown before automatically entering KEEP WARM mode and starting the counting up.

7. To quickly discharge the pressurized steam, turn the pressure release valve to the VENT position. The pressure release valve will discharge a blast of steam. The float valve will drop after all of the steam has been released, allowing the lid to be opened.

Steam

1. The reversible rack or Cook & Crisp Basket with ingredients should be placed in the pot after adding 250 ml of liquid (or the quantity suggested by the recipe).

2. Turn the pressure release valve to the VENT position after installing the pressure lid.

3. Press FUNCTION, then choose STEAM using the START/STOP dial.

4. To change the cooking time in minute increments up to 30 minutes, press TIME and then turn the dial. To start or stop cooking, press START/STOP.

5. To get the liquid to boil, the machine will start preheating. PRE will

appear on the screen. The preheating image will play until the appliance reaches the desired temperature, at which point BOIL will appear on the display and the timer will start to clock down.

6. The appliance will automatically switch to Keep Warm mode and start counting up once the cooking time is up by beeping. Before opening the lid, be sure the float valve has descended.

Slow Cook

1. Add all components to the pot. The pot should not be filled past the MAX line.

2. Turn the pressure release valve to the VENT position after installing the pressure lid.

3. Press FUNCTION, then choose SLOW COOK using the START/STOP dial. It will show the current temperature setting. To choose HI or LO, spin the dial after pressing TEMP.

4. Press TIME, then spin the dial to change the cooking time up to 12 hours in 15-minute intervals.

6 | Fundamentals of Ninja Foodi Max Multi-Cooker

5. To start or stop cooking, press START/STOP.
6. The appliance will beep, go into Keep Warm mode, and start counting up once the cooking time is up.

Yogurt

1. Add milk to the saucepan in the required quantity.
2. Turn the pressure release valve to the VENT position after installing the pressure lid.
3. To choose YOGURT, spin the START/STOP dial after pressing FUNCTION. It will show the current temperature setting. Press TEMP, then choose YGRT or FMNT using the dial.
4. Press TIME, and then move the dial to change the incubation time between 8 and 12 hours in 30-minute intervals.
5. To start pasteurization, press START/STOP. 6 While pasteurizing, the unit will display "BOIL." The device will beep and indicate "COOL" when the pasteurization temperature has been reached.
6. The device will show ADD and STIR in sequence along with the incubation period after the milk has cooled.
7. Remove the pressure lid, then skim the milk's surface.
8. Stir milk and yogurt cultures together. To start the incubation process, attach the pressure lid and click START/STOP.
9. The countdown will start after FMNT appears on the display. The device will beep and display DONE when the incubation period is finished. Until it is turned off, the device will beep once per minute for up to four

hours.

10. Up to 12 hours before serving, chill yogurt.

Sear/Sauté

1. Add ingredients to the pot.
2. Select SEAR/SAUTÉ by turning the dial after pressing FUNCTION. It will show the current temperature setting. Press TEMP, then choose LO, LO: MD, MD, MD: HI, or HI by rotating the dial.
3. To start or stop cooking, press START/STOP.
4. To switch off the SEAR/SAUTÉ feature, press START/STOP. Press FUNCTION, then rotate the START/STOP dial to the appropriate cooking function to change the cooking function.

Pressure Release Options

Natural Pressure Release: As the appliance cools down after pressure cooking is finished, steam will naturally escape from it. Depending on the number of components in the pot, this might take up to 20 minutes. The appliance will then enter the Keep Warm mode. If you want to exit Keep Warm mode, press KEEP WARM. The float valve will descend when the whole natural pressure release has occurred.

Only use a quick pressure release if your recipe specifies it. Turn the pressure release valve to the VENT position to swiftly release the steam after pressure cooking and the KEEP WARM light turns on. An audible hiss will be present when steam is released. After the pressure is released, some steam will still be within the appliance, but it will eventually leak when the lid is opened. Make sure there are no condensation drips in the stove base when you lift and tilt it away from you.

Extra Accessories for Perfect Cooking in Ninja Foodi Max Multi-Cooker:

1. Cooking Pot: An additional pot to continue the Foodi® fun when your primary pot is already brimming with delectable food.
2. Multi-Purpose Silicone Sling: Easily pull ingredients and pans into and out of the cooking pot with the Multi-Purpose Silicone Sling.
3. Multi-Purpose Tin: Bake a fluffy, moist cake with a golden top for dessert, or make casseroles, dips, and sweet or savory pies. H6cm D22cm.
4. Folding Crisping Rack: Make taco

8 | Fundamentals of Ninja Foodi Max Multi-Cooker

shells out of tortillas or cook a complete package of bacon.

5. Our particularly sized loaf pan is the ideal baking tool for bread mixtures like banana and courgette. approx. L21cm x W11cm x H9cm.
6. Glass lid: Use it to effortlessly carry or store food while cooking and to see inside the pot.
7. Additional Pack of Silicone Rings: Use one silicone ring while cooking savory meals and the other when cooking sweet items to help maintain flavours distinct.
8. Skewer Stand: Only the 7.5L variants are compatible with the skewer stand. Make kebabs with the skewer stand. Included are 15 skewers.

Cleaning

- After each usage, the appliance has to be completely cleaned.
- Before cleaning, unplug the device from the electrical socket.
- Wipe a moist towel over the control panel and stove base to clean them.
- Dishwasher-safe items include the pressure lid, cooking pot, silicone ring, reversible rack, Cook & Crisp Basket, and detachable diffuser.
- The anti-clog cap and pressure release valve may be cleaned with water and dish soap.
- After the heat shield has cooled, clean the crisping lid by wiping it down with a wet cloth or paper towel.
- Fill the pot with water and let it soak before cleaning if food residue is stuck to the cooking pot, reversible rack, or Cook & Crisp Basket. AVOID using scouring pads. If scrubbing is required, use a nylon pad or brush with liquid dish soap or non-abrasive cleaner.
- After each usage, let all pieces air dry.

Taking Off and Replacing the Silicone Ring

- Pull the silicone ring piece by section outward from the silicone ring rack to remove it. Either side of the ring can be mounted facing upward. Section by section, push it into the rack to

reinstall. Remove any food particles from the silicone ring and anti-clog cap after use.
- To prevent odor, keep the silicone ring clean. The smell may be eliminated by washing it in the dishwasher or warm, soapy water. It is nonetheless typical for it to take in the aroma of some acidic meals. It is advised to keep several silicone rings on hand.
- NEVER take the silicone ring out too forcefully as this might damage the rack and the pressure-sealing ability. Replace any silicone ring that has cracks, cuts, or other damage right away.

Frequently Asked Questions

1. Why does it take my unit so long to reach pressure? How long does it take for pressure to build?

- Depending on the chosen temperature, the cooking pot's current temperature, and the temperature or amount of the contents, cooking durations may vary.
- Make sure your silicone ring is flat with the lid and properly placed. If placed properly, you should be able to spin the ring by giving it a small tug.
- When pressure cooking, make sure the pressure lid is completely closed and the pressure release valve is in the SEAL position.

2. Why does the clock go so slowly?

- Instead of setting minutes, you may have done so. When setting the time, the display will read HH: MM and the time will advance or backward by minutes.

3. How can I detect whether the appliance is under pressure?

- As the device builds pressure, whirling lights will show up on the screen. When utilizing the pressure or steam

10 | Fundamentals of Ninja Foodi Max Multi-Cooker

function, PRE and moving lights are displayed on the display screen.
- When utilizing STEAM or PRESSURE, this shows that the unit is building pressure or preheating. Your designated cook time will start to run out once the machine has completed creating pressure.
- It's usual for steam to leak through the pressure release valve while cooking.
- There is a lot of steam coming from my device when utilizing the Steam feature. For steam, slow cooking, and sear/sauté, keep the pressure release valve in the VENT position.

4. Why am I unable to remove the pressure lid?
- The pressure cover won't unlock as a safety measure until the device is fully depressurized. To quickly discharge the pressurized steam, turn the pressure release valve to the VENT position. Steam will suddenly erupt from the pressure release valve. The appliance will be prepared to open after all of the steam has been released. Turn the pressure lid counterclockwise, then lift the lid at an angle to prevent splatter. Do not lift the lid straight up.

5. Is the pressure release valve supposed to be loose?
- Yes. The loose fit of the pressure release valve is deliberate; it makes it simple to switch from SEAL to VENT and helps manage pressure

by releasing a tiny quantity of steam while cooking to provide excellent results. For pressure cooking, please make sure it is turned as far as possible toward the SEAL position, and for rapid releasing, please make sure it is turned as far as possible toward the VENT position. The appliance hisses and cannot build pressure. A pressure release valve should be switched to the SEAL setting, so double-check this. If, after doing this, if you still hear a loud hissing sound, your silicone seal might not be installed completely. To stop cooking, press START/STOP, vent as required, and take off the pressure cover. Make sure the silicone ring is properly placed and flatly underneath the ring rack by applying pressure to it. Once everything is in place, you ought to be able to spin the ring by giving it a gentle tug. Instead of ticking down, the device is counting up.
- The appliance is in Keep Warm mode after the cooking cycle has finished.

Fundamentals of Ninja Foodi Max Multi-Cooker | 11

6. **How much time does it take the unit to depressurize?**
- A quick release lasts no more than two minutes. Depending on the type of food, amount of liquid, and/or combination of food and liquid in the pot, natural release can take up to 20 minutes or more.

7. **The error message "ADD POT" displays on the monitor.**
- The cooker base does not contain the cooking pot. Every function requires a cooking pot.

8. **The error message "OTHR LID" and the lid icon flash on the display screen.**
- The wrong lid is attached for the cooking operation you want. To utilize the Pressure, Slow Cook, Yogurt, Steam, or Keep Warm features, install the pressure lid.

9. **The error message "SHUT LID" shows on the monitor.**
- The desired function cannot begin because the crisping lid is open.

10. **The error message "TURN LID" displays on the monitor.**
- The pressure lid's installation is incomplete. To utilize the pressure, slow cook, yogurt, steam, and keep warm features, turn the pressure knob clockwise until it clicks.

11. **The problem message "OPEN VENT" displays on the display panel.**
- The pressure release valve is in the SEAL position when the device is set to Slow Cook or Sear/Sauté and detects pressure building up.
- For the duration of the cooking operation, turn the pressure release valve to the VENT position and leave it there.
- The program will end and the device will switch off if the pressure release valve is not turned to the VENT position in the allotted time of five

minutes.

12. When utilizing the Steam feature, a notice titled "ADD WATR" shows on the screen.

- The water is not deep enough. To keep the device functioning, add extra water.

13. An error message with the text "ADD WATR" appears on the screen while using the Pressure function.

- Before starting the pressure cook cycle again, add extra liquid to the cooking pot.
- A pressure release valve should be in the SEAL position.
- Verify that the silicone ring is properly fitted.

Cooking Tips and Warnings

1. For uniform browning, ensure sure components are layered evenly and without overlap in the bottom of the cooking pot. If components overlap, shake the pan halfway during the cooking period.
2. We advise first wrapping tiny items in a parchment paper or foil bag if they could fall through the reversible rack.
3. For maximum crisping results, it is advised to drain the pot of any liquid before switching from pressure cooking to using the crisping cover.
4. After cooking, maintain food at a warm, safe temperature by using the Keep Warm option. We advise keeping the lid on and using this feature right before serving to avoid food drying out. Use the Air Crisp option to reheat food and NEVER use the socket under the counter.
5. NEVER attach this appliance to a separate remote control or timer switch.
6. If the plug or power cable is damaged, do not use the appliance. Stop using the appliance right away and contact customer service if it has any problems or has been damaged in any way.
7. To protect yourself from steam and hot liquids, ALWAYS tilt the lid so that it is between your body and the inside pot.
8. ALWAYS make sure the appliance is installed correctly before using it.
9. Always inspect the red float valve and pressure release valve for blockage or clogging before using, and clean them if required. Verify that the pressure

Fundamentals of Ninja Foodi Max Multi-Cooker | 13

lid's red float valve can move easily. When cooked under pressure, foods like apple sauce, cranberries, pearl barley, oatmeal or other cereals, split peas, noodles, macaroni, rhubarb, or spaghetti may foam, froth, or sputter, blocking the pressure release valve.

10. NEVER use the SLOW COOK option if there is no food or liquid in the detachable cooking pot.
11. The use of the device without the cooking pot is not recommended.
12. DO NOT deep fried anything in this appliance.
13. The pressure valves MUST NOT be covered.
14. While pressure cooking, AVOID using oil for sautéing or frying.
15. Keep food away from hot sources. When cooking, DO NOT overfill or go over the MAX load level. Overfilling might endanger users' safety, result in property damage, or render the appliance unsafe.
16. DO NOT overfill the Cook &

Crisp Basket to keep food from coming into touch with the heating components.
17. Close the crisping lid very carefully to avoid trapping anything in the hinge or getting it hooked.
18. Different socket voltages may have an impact on how well your product functions. Use a thermometer to ensure that your food is prepared to the proper temperatures to avoid any potential illnesses.
19. When operating, DO NOT position the appliance close to a worktop edge.
20. Avoid using metal scouring pads when cleaning. An electric shock risk exists if broken pieces of the pad come into contact with electrical components.
21. NEVER handle kitchen utensils while cooking or just after.

4-Week Meal Plan

Week 1

Day 1
Breakfast: Cheese Sausage and Egg Strata
Lunch: Cheese Pasta with Broccoli
Dinner: Beef and Carrot Stew with Bacon
Dessert: Cheesecake with Peaches

Day 2
Breakfast: Banana-Nutella Stuffed French Toast
Lunch: Cheesy Tortellini Alfredo and Peas
Dinner: Teriyaki Chicken Wings
Dessert: Vanilla Cheesecake

Day 3
Breakfast: Breakfast Farro with Apricots
Lunch: Salmon, Leek, and Potato Soup
Dinner: Curried Prawns with Vegetables & Rice Vermicelli
Dessert: Delicious Maple Crème Brule

Day 4
Breakfast: Steel-Cut Oats with Dried Apples
Lunch: Lemony Mushroom and Leeks Risotto
Dinner: Homemade Beef & Beets Borscht
Dessert: Homemade Molten Mocha Cake

Day 5
Breakfast: Creamy Polenta
Lunch: White Rice with Peas and Swiss Chard
Dinner: Tasty Barbecue Chicken–Stuffed Sweet Potatoes
Dessert: Classic Cheesecake

Day 6
Breakfast: Quinoa Chili with Feta cheese
Lunch: Pearled Barley-Lentil Soup with Spinach
Dinner: Creamy Seafood and Noodles Casserole
Dessert: Peach-Berry Cobbler

Day 7
Breakfast: Honey Veggie Corn Muffins
Lunch: Mustard Potato and Bacon Salad
Dinner: Lemony Beef Risotto
Dessert: Caramel Brownie Pudding

Week 2

Day 1
Breakfast: Tasty Courgette & Cheese Drop Biscuits
Lunch: Spiced Yellow Lentil and Spinach Soup
Dinner: Indian Curried Chicken
Dessert: Best Key Lime Pie

Day 2
Breakfast: Rosemary Apricot Scones
Lunch: Simple Corn on the Cob (Four Ways)
Dinner: Coffee-Rubbed Steak and Rice Bowls
Dessert: Vanilla Lemon Cheesecake

Day 3
Breakfast: Garlic Cheese Bread
Lunch: Indian-Spiced Basmati Rice with Peas
Dinner: Lamb and Carrot Stew
Dessert: Easy White Chocolate Pots De Crème

Day 4:
Breakfast: Jalapeño-Cheddar Bagel Egg Casserole
Lunch: Spiced Red Lentil and Pumpkin Soup
Dinner: Cheese and Courgette Stuffed Chicken
Dessert: Delicious Stuffed Peaches

Day 5:
Breakfast: Homemade Gingerbread French Toast Casserole
Lunch: Spanish Rice with Peppers
Dinner: Herbed Beef & Cheddar Croissants
Dessert: Carrot Coconut Cake with Pecans

Day 6:
Breakfast: Chocolate Banana Bread
Lunch: Cheesy Spaghetti with Sausage and Broccolini
Dinner: Cranberry Hot Chicken Wings
Dessert: Lemony Tapioca Pudding

Day 7:
Breakfast: Mushroom Congee Breakfast Bowl
Lunch: Lima Beans with Bacon & Tomato
Dinner: Chili Beef Hot Dog Soup
Dessert: Red Wine-Braised Apples

Week 3

Day 1
Breakfast: Spicy Pork Chorizo with Mexican Eggs
Lunch: Spiced Corn with Jalapeno-Peppers
Dinner: Lemony Chicken with Artichoke Avocado
Dessert: Cranberry & Walnuts Stuffed Apples

Day 2
Breakfast: Creamy Strawberry Oats
Lunch: Kale and Edamame Salad with Sesame Ginger Dressing
Dinner: Easy Beef and Broccoli
Dessert: Chocolate-Berry Mug Cake

Day 3
Breakfast: Israeli Couscous and Veggie
Lunch: Jalapeno & Cotija Cheese Potato Pie
Dinner: Cumin Salsa Verde Chicken
Dessert: Delicious Stuffed Peaches

Day 4
Breakfast: Buckwheat Banana Porridge
Lunch: Rosemary Navy Beans
Dinner: Beef and Sausage Soup with Pepperoni
Dessert: Vanilla Cheesecake

Day 5
Breakfast: Banana-Walnuts Oatmeal
Lunch: Cheese Broccoli Potato Cake
Dinner: Smoked Paprika Turkey Lunchmeat
Dessert: Delicious Maple Crème Brule

Day 6
Breakfast: Cheese Sausage and Egg Strata
Lunch: Sweet Potato Lentil Soup with Spinach
Dinner: Pulled Beef with Pappardelle
Dessert: Homemade Molten Mocha Cake

Day 7
Breakfast: Banana-Nutella Stuffed French Toast
Lunch: Black Bean and Rice–Stuffed Peppers
Dinner: Cajun Chicken and Rice Bowls
Dessert: Cheesecake with Peaches

Week 4

Day 1
Breakfast: Breakfast Farro with Apricots
Lunch: Cheesy Alfredo Pasta with Carrots & Broccoli
Dinner: Garlicky Pork Roast with Red Cabbage
Dessert: Classic Cheesecake

Day 2
Breakfast: Steel-Cut Oats with Dried Apples
Lunch: Black Bean & Brown Rice Casserole
Dinner: Beef, Barley and Celery Soup
Dessert: Peach-Berry Cobbler

Day 3
Breakfast: Creamy Polenta
Lunch: Vegetarian Gumbo with Rice
Dinner: Spiced Mango-Chipotle Shredded Chicken
Dessert: Caramel Brownie Pudding

Day 4
Breakfast: Quinoa Chili with Feta cheese
Lunch: Autumn Potatoes Egg Salad
Dinner: Beer-Braised Pork with Sauerkraut
Dessert: Best Key Lime Pie

Day 5
Breakfast: Honey Veggie Corn Muffins
Lunch: White Rice with Peas and Swiss Chard
Dinner: French Onion Cheese Chicken
Dessert: Vanilla Lemon Cheesecake

Day 6
Breakfast: Tasty Courgette & Cheese Drop Biscuits
Lunch: Lima Beans with Bacon & Tomato
Dinner: Pork Chops with Creamy Mushroom Gravy
Dessert: Easy White Chocolate Pots De Crème

Day 7
Breakfast: Rosemary Apricot Scones
Lunch: Lemony Mushroom and Leeks Risotto
Dinner: Creamy Curry Chicken Bites
Dessert: Carrot Coconut Cake with Pecans

Chapter 1 Breakfast Recipes

Chocolate Banana Bread

Prep time: 20 minutes | **Cook time:** 55 minutes | **Serves:** 8-10

8 tbsp grass-fed butter, ghee or avocado oil, melted, plus more for casserole dish
140 g pure maple syrup
3 small ripe bananas, quartered
2 large eggs, at room temperature
1 tsp pure vanilla extract
125 g cassava flour
25 g unsweetened cocoa powder
25 g grass-fed hydrolyzed collagen
1 tsp baking soda
½ tsp sea salt
140 g chopped quality chocolate
240 ml water

1. Grease a casserole dish that fits inside the Ninja XL Pressure Cooker. Line the bottom of the casserole dish with a circle of parchment paper. Set aside. 2. In a blender, in the order listed, place all the ingredients, except the chopped chocolate and water. 3. Mix on low speed until smooth and fully combined, about 20 seconds, scraping down the sides, if needed. Add the chopped chocolate to the blender and give it a stir with a spatula to fold in. 4. Pour the batter into the prepared casserole dish. Cover the casserole dish with its glass lid. If your casserole dish doesn't come with a glass lid, you can cover the top of the dish with unbleached parchment paper, then top it with foil and secure it around the edges. 5. Pour the water into the pot and place the bottom layer of the Deluxe Reversible Rack in the lower position. Carefully set the covered casserole dish on top of the rack. Close the lid and move slider to PRESSURE. Ensuring the pressure release valve is in the SEAL position. The temperature will default to HIGH, which is the correct setting. Set time to 55 minutes. Select START/STOP to begin cooking. 6. When cooking is complete, allow the unit to release pressure naturally for 20 minutes. Using an oven mitt, do a quick release, then carefully open the lid. 7. Carefully lift the casserole dish out of the pot. Use oven mitts or towels because the unit and dish will be extremely hot. 8. Test with a toothpick to make sure the centre is fully cooked; no more than a few moist crumbs should be on the toothpick. 9. If it needs more time, re-cover with the lid (make sure to wipe off any condensation first) and return to the pot to cook on PRESSURE function for another 5 minutes, then do a quick pressure release. 10. Allow the bread to cool at room temperature on a cooling rack for 45 minutes. Gently run a knife around the edges of the bread to loosen it when you're ready to remove it from the dish. 11. Turn the dish upside down on a plate to release the banana bread. Cut the banana bread into thick slices and serve immediately.
Per Serving: Calories 338; Fat 14.36g; Sodium 741mg; Carbs 51.93g; Fibre 2.9g; Sugar 31.84g; Protein 2.87g

Cheese Sausage and Egg Strata

Prep time: 10 minutes | **Cook time:** 21 minutes | **Serves:** 6

5 English muffins, toasted and torn into 2.5 cm pieces	300 ml milk
1 tablespoon olive oil	3 tablespoons chopped fresh chives
300 g pork or turkey breakfast sausage	Salt and freshly ground black pepper
6 large eggs	75 g grated cheddar cheese

1. Spray a round metal baking pan with that will fit in the pot with cooking spray. Place the English muffin pieces in the pan; set aside. 2. Put the oil in the pot, move slider to AIR FRY/STOVETOP. Select SEAR/SAUTÉ and set to 3. Select START/STOP to begin preheating. Allow unit to preheat for 5 minutes. 3. When the oil is hot, add the sausage and cook, breaking it up into large pieces with a spatula, until cooked through, 6 minutes. Press START/STOP to stop cooking. Pour out the sausage onto a paper towel–lined plate. Return the pot to the appliance. 4. In a bowl, combine the eggs, milk, chives, ½ teaspoon salt, and several grinds of pepper and whisk well. 5. Slowly pour the egg mixture over the English muffins, lightly pressing down on the bread so it absorbs the custard. Sprinkle the sausage and cheese evenly over the top; press again to submerge most of the bread in the custard. Cover with foil. 6. Pour 360 ml cold water into the pot. Then place the bottom layer of the Deluxe Reversible Rack in the lower position in the pot. Place the muffins with foil on the rack. Close the lid and move the slider to PRESSURE. Ensuring the pressure release valve is in the SEAL position. The temperature will default to HIGH, which is the correct setting. Set time to 15 minutes. Select START/STOP to begin cooking. 7. When cooking is complete, release the pressure quickly by turning the pressure release valve to the VENT position. Move slider to the right to unlock the lid. 8. Insert a butter knife into the centre of the strata; it should come out with no liquid custard coating the knife. 9. If the pudding is not done, lock on the lid and return to HIGH pressure for 1 minute more. Quick-release the pressure. 10. Remove the strata from the pot and serve right away.

Per Serving: Calories 348; Fat 18.93g; Sodium 818mg; Carbs 27.39g; Fibre 2.2g; Sugar 3.52g; Protein 17.29g

Banana–Walnuts Oatmeal

Prep time: 10 minutes | **Cook time:** 10 minutes | **Serves:** 2-4

2 ripe bananas, mashed	1 tsp vanilla
80 g steel cut oatmeal	¼ tsp salt
720 ml water	60 g walnuts, chopped
¼ tsp nutmeg	70 g honey
1 tsp cinnamon	

1. With a potato masher or a fork, mash the bananas at the bottom of the pot. 2. Add the oats, water, cinnamon, vanilla, nutmeg, and salt and stir. 3. Close and secure the lid. Move slider to PRESSURE and Ensuring the pressure release valve is in the SEAL position. The temperature will default to HIGH, which is the correct setting. Set time to 10 minutes. Select START/STOP to begin cooking. 4. When cooking is complete, release the pressure quickly by turning the pressure release valve to the VENT position. Move slider to the right to unlock the lid, then carefully open it. 5. Stir in the walnuts and honey. The oatmeal will continue to thicken as it cools. Serve.

Per Serving: Calories 386; Fat 11.13g; Sodium 337mg; Carbs 71.38g; Fibre 6.8g; Sugar 39.44g; Protein 6.89g

Banana–Nutella Stuffed French Toast

Prep time: 10 minutes | **Cook time:** 20 minutes | **Serves:** 6

8 (1 cm-thick) slices challah bread (200 g)
150 g chocolate hazelnut spread (such as Nutella)
2 large medium-ripe bananas, sliced
360 ml milk
3 large eggs

1. Thoroughly coat a 18 × 10 cm round metal baking pan with cooking spray. Then place the bottom layer of the Deluxe Reversible Rack in the lower position in the pot and add 360 ml cold water. 2. Spread one side of each slice of bread with chocolate-hazelnut spread. Layer the bread and bananas in the prepared baking dish in two layers, ending with bananas. 3. In a medium bowl, combine the milk and eggs, whisk until well blended. Pour the milk mixture evenly over the bread layers in the pan and press down gently so the bread absorbs the custard. 4. Cover the baking pan tightly with foil. Set the baking pan on the rack in the pot. Close the lid and move slider to PRESSURE. Ensuring the pressure release valve is in the SEAL position. The temperature will default to HIGH, which is the correct setting. Set time to 20 minutes. Select START/STOP to begin cooking. 5. When the cooking time is up, let the pressure come down naturally for 10 minutes and then quick-release the remaining pressure. 6. To check if the banana and hazelnut spread casserole is ready, insert a butter knife into the centre of the dish. The knife should come out moist, but without any liquid custard on it. Although the top may appear moist initially, let it sit at room temperature for a few minutes to allow it to become slightly firmer before serving. 7. If the casserole is not yet cooked, put the lid back on and cook it under HIGH pressure for another minute before quick-releasing the pressure.
Per Serving: Calories 178; Fat 6.34g; Sodium 225mg; Carbs 23.21g; Fibre 1.2g; Sugar 6.51g; Protein 6.71g

Breakfast Farro with Apricots

Prep time: 20 minutes | **Cook time:** 15 minutes | **Serves:** 6

2 tablespoons salted butter
85 g pearled farro
1 teaspoon ground cardamom
95 g dried apricots, chopped
½ teaspoon salt
Honey, to serve
Yogurt, to serve

1. Add the butter to the Ninja XL Pressure Cooker. Move slider to AIR FRY/STOVETOP. Select SEAR/SAUTÉ and set to 3. Select START/STOP to begin preheating. Allow unit to preheat for 5 minutes. 2. When the butter is melted, add the farro and cardamom, then cook, stirring occasionally, until fragrant and toasted, about 3 minutes. Stir in 840 ml water, the apricots and salt, then distribute in an even layer. 3. Close the lid and move slider to PRESSURE. Ensuring the pressure release valve is in the SEAL position. The temperature will default to HIGH, which is the correct setting. Set time to 12 minutes. Select START/STOP to begin cooking. 4. When cooking is complete, release the pressure quickly by turning the pressure release valve to the VENT position. Move slider to the right to unlock the lid, then carefully open it. 5. Stir the mixture well, then re-cover without locking the lid in place. Let stand for 10 minutes. Stir vigorously until thick and creamy, about 30 seconds. 6. Serve with honey and yogurt.
Per Serving: Calories 232; Fat 3.23g; Sodium 221mg; Carbs 47.32g; Fibre 8.7g; Sugar 7.63g; Protein 5.49g

Steel-Cut Oats with Dried Apples

Prep time: 15 minutes | **Cook time:** 10 minutes | **Serves:** 6

2 tablespoons salted butter
120 g steel-cut oats
½ teaspoon ground allspice
95 g dried apples, chopped
½ teaspoon salt
Maple syrup or brown sugar, to serve
Milk or cream, to serve

1. Add the butter to the Ninja XL Pressure Cooker. Move slider to AIR FRY/STOVETOP. Select SEAR/SAUTÉ and set to 3. Select START/STOP to begin preheating. Allow unit to preheat for 5 minutes. 2. Stir the butter occasionally until it begins to smell nutty and the milk solids at the bottom begin to brown, about 3 minutes. 3. Stir in the oats and allspice, then cook, stirring often, until fragrant and toasted, about 3 minutes. Add 1.3 L water, the apples and salt; stir to combine, then distribute in an even layer. 4. Press START/STOP to turn off the SEAR/SAUTÉ function, close the lid and move slider to PRESSURE. Ensuring the pressure release valve is in the SEAL position. The temperature will default to HIGH, which is the correct setting. Set time to 5 minutes. Select START/STOP to begin cooking. 5. When cooking is complete, release the pressure quickly by turning the pressure release valve to the VENT position. Move slider to the right to unlock the lid, then carefully open it. 6. Stir the mixture well, then re-cover without locking the lid in place. Let rest for 10 minutes. Stir vigorously until thick and creamy, about 30 seconds. 7. Serve with maple syrup and milk.
Per Serving: Calories 99; Fat 4.63g; Sodium 225mg; Carbs 18.71g; Fibre 3.9g; Sugar 3.11g; Protein 4.8g

Creamy Polenta

Prep time: 10 minutes | **Cook time:** 6½ hours | **Serves:** 4

240g coarse stoneground yellow polenta
Salt and ground black pepper

1. Add 1.8 L water, the polenta and 2½ teaspoons salt to Ninja XL Pressure Cooker. 2. Close the lid and move slider to PRESSURE. Ensuring the pressure release valve is in the SEAL position. The temperature will default to HIGH, which is the correct setting. Set time to 20 minutes. Select START/STOP to begin cooking. 3. When pressure cooking is complete, let the pressure reduce naturally for 20 minutes, then release the remaining steam by moving the pressure valve to Venting. Move slider to the right to unlock the lid, then carefully open it. 4. Then Select SEAR/SAUTÉ and set to 3. Bring the mixture to a simmer, stirring often. Press START/STOP, lock the lid in place and move the pressure valve to Venting. 5. Select Slow Cook and set the temperature to Lo. Set the cooking time for 6 hours. Press START/STOP to begin cooking, then carefully open the pot. 6. Whisk the polenta until creamy, then taste and season with salt and pepper. Let stand for about 10 minutes to thicken slightly, then stir again and serve.
Per Serving: Calories 222; Fat 1.05g; Sodium 5mg; Carbs 47.84g; Fibre 2.5g; Sugar 1.52g; Protein 4.41g

Quinoa Chili with Feta cheese

Prep time: 30 minutes | **Cook time:** 6½ hours | **Serves:** 4 to 6

3 tablespoons rapeseed oil
1 medium yellow onion, finely chopped
4 medium garlic cloves, smashed and peeled
3 plum tomatoes, cored and chopped
Salt and ground black pepper
1 yellow pepper, stemmed, seeded and chopped
1 habanero chili, halved
2½ teaspoons sweet paprika
2½ teaspoons ground cumin
1 teaspoon dried oregano
255 g red, white or tricolour (rainbow) quinoa, rinsed and drained
100 g feta cheese, cut into 1 cm cubes
Chopped fresh coriander, to serve

1. Select sear/sauté function of your Ninja XL Pressure Cooker and set to lo1, heat the oil until shimmering. 2. Add the onion, tomatoes, garlic, 1½ teaspoons salt and ¼ teaspoon pepper. Cook, stirring occasionally, until the moisture evaporates and the onion is softened and translucent, about 10 minutes. 3. Add the pepper, paprika, chili, cumin and oregano, then cook, stirring frequently, until the spices begin to stick to the bottom of the pot, 1 to 2 minutes. 4. Stir in the quinoa and 480 ml water, scraping up any browned bits; distribute the mixture in an even layer. 5. Close the lid and move slider to PRESSURE. Ensuring the pressure release valve is in the SEAL position. Adjust the pressure level to low. Set time to 12 minutes. Select START/STOP to begin cooking. 6. When pressure cooking is complete, let the pressure reduce naturally for 10 minutes, then release the remaining steam by moving the pressure valve to venting. Press START/STOP, then carefully open the pot. 7. Fluff the quinoa with a fork, removing and discarding the chili halves. Add the feta cheese and stir until it begins to melt. Stir in 480 ml water and re-cover without locking the lid in place, then let stand for 5 minutes. 8. Select SEAR/SAUTÉ function, bring the mixture to a boil. Press START/STOP to begin cooking, lock the lid in place and move the pressure valve to venting. Select slow cook and set the temperature to Lo. Set the cooking time for 6 hours; the mixture is done when the quinoa has absorbed the liquid. 9. Season with salt and pepper. Sprinkle with coriander and serve.
Per Serving: Calories 248; Fat 15.61g; Sodium 330mg; Carbs 23.65g; Fibre 2.3g; Sugar 15.2g; Protein 6.46g

Buckwheat Banana Porridge

Prep time: 10 minutes | **Cook time:** 6 minutes | **Serves:** 4

135 g raw buckwheat groats
720 ml rice milk
1 banana, sliced
30 g raisins
1 tsp ground cinnamon
½ tsp vanilla
Chopped nuts, optional

1. Rinse the buckwheat well and put in the pot of your Ninja XL Pressure Cooker. 2. Add the rice milk, raisins, banana, cinnamon and vanilla. 3. Close the lid and move slider to PRESSURE. Ensuring the pressure release valve is in the SEAL position. The temperature will default to HIGH, which is the correct setting. Set time to 6 minutes. Select START/STOP to begin cooking. 4. Once cooking is complete, use a Natural Release for 20 minutes, then release any remaining pressure. 5. Open the lid and stir the porridge. If you like, you can sprinkle with chopped nuts.
Per Serving: Calories 194; Fat 7.45g; Sodium 81mg; Carbs 25.22g; Fibre 2.3g; Sugar 13.47g; Protein 8g

Honey Veggie Corn Muffins

Prep time: 10 minutes | **Cook time:** 15 minutes | **Serves:** 12

145 g yellow polenta
65 g flour
65 g whole wheat flour
1 tsp. baking powder
¾ tsp. salt
1 large egg

240 ml unsweetened almond milk
60 ml rapeseed oil
70 g honey
60 g finely shredded carrot
75 g finely chopped green pepper

1. Coat 12 muffin cups with cooking spray. 2. Combine the polenta, flours, baking powder and salt in a bowl. In a separate bowl, mix together egg, milk, oil and honey. Add to polenta mixture; stir just until moistened. Fold in the vegetables. Fill prepared cups two-thirds full. 3. Place the muffin cups on the bottom layer of the Deluxe Reversible Rack in the lower position, then place the rack in the pot. 4. Close the lid and make sure the slider is in the AIR FRY/STOVETOP. Select BAKE/ROAST, set temperature to 205°C, and set time to 15 minutes. Select START/STOP to begin cooking. 5. Bake until a toothpick inserted in centre comes out clean. Let Cool for 5 minutes before removing from the rack. Serve warm.
Per Serving: Calories 172; Fat 6.05g; Sodium 193mg; Carbs 27.17g; Fibre 1.7g; Sugar 7.3g; Protein 3.28g

Spicy Pork Chorizo with Mexican Eggs

Prep time: 10 minutes | **Cook time:** 20 minutes | **Serves:** 4-6

1 tbsp extra-virgin olive oil
1 small russet potato, diced
2 tomatillos, husked, washed and diced
1 yellow onion, diced
1 jalapeño pepper, minced
200 g ground pork chorizo
½ tsp ground cumin

½ tsp smoked paprika
Salt
Freshly ground black pepper
215 g salsa verde
240 ml low-sodium chicken stock
4 to 6 large eggs

1. Add the olive oil to the pot of your Ninja XL Pressure Cooker. Move slider to AIR FRY/STOVETOP functions. Select SEAR/SAUTÉ and set temperature to 2. Wait 1 minute for the oil to heat up and then add the potato, tomatillos, onion, jalapeño and chorizo. Sauté for 5 minutes, stirring occasionally. 2. Stir in the cumin, paprika and salt and black pepper to taste. Sauté for an additional minute. Press START/STOP to turn off the SEAR/SAUTÉ function. 3. Stir in the salsa verde and stock and be sure to scrape up any browned bits from the bottom of the pot. 4. Close the lid and move slider to PRESSURE. Ensuring the pressure release valve is in the SEAL position. The temperature will default to HIGH, which is the correct setting. Set time to 4 minutes. Select START/STOP to begin cooking. 5. When cooking is complete, release the pressure quickly by turning the pressure release valve to the VENT position. Move slider to the right to unlock the lid, then carefully open it. 6. Give the mixture a quick stir. Move slider to AIR FRY/STOVETOP functions. Select SEAR/SAUTÉ and set to Hi 5. 7. Crack the eggs into the salsa verde mixture, leaving about 2.5 cm between each egg. Season the top of each egg with a little bit of salt and pepper. 8. Sauté for about 10 minutes, or until the white part of the egg is no longer translucent.
Per Serving: Calories 303; Fat 13.81g; Sodium 695mg; Carbs 23.07g; Fibre 3.2g; Sugar 6.07g; Protein 23.5g

Tasty Courgette & Cheese Drop Biscuits

Prep time: 25 minutes | **Cook time:** 25 minutes | **Serves:** 12

- 90 g shredded courgette
- 1¼ tsp. salt, divided
- 185 g plain flour
- 1 tbsp. baking powder
- 115 g cold butter, cubed
- 50 g shredded cheddar cheese
- 30 g shredded part-skim mozzarella cheese
- 25 g shredded Parmesan cheese
- 2 tbsp. finely chopped oil-packed sun-dried tomatoes, patted dry
- 2 tbsp. minced fresh basil or 2 tsp. dried basil
- 240 ml low fat milk

1. Put the courgette in a strainer on top of a plate, add ¼ tsp salt, and mix. 2. Leave it for 10 minutes, then rinse it and drain it well. Squeeze the courgette to get rid of any excess liquid, and dry it with a paper towel. 3. In a big bowl, mix together the flour, baking powder, and the rest of the salt. Cut in the butter until the mixture looks like coarse crumbs. Add the courgette, cheeses, tomatoes, and basil, and stir everything together. 4. Finally, pour in the milk and mix everything until it's just moistened. Drop by scant spoonfuls into a greased baking pan that can fit the pot. 5. Place the pan on the bottom layer of the Deluxe Reversible Rack in the lower position. 6. When the pot has preheated, place the rack with pan in the pot. Close the lid and make sure the slider is in the AIR FRY/STOVETOP. Select BAKE/ROAST, set temperature to 205°C, and set time to 25 minutes. Select START/STOP to begin cooking. Bake golden brown. 7. Serve warm.

Per Serving: Calories 196; Fat 9.85g; Sodium 371mg; Carbs 22g; Fibre 0.8g; Sugar 1.2g; Protein 4.84g

Israeli Couscous and Veggie

Prep time: 10 minutes | **Cook time:** 6 minutes | **Serves:** 4-6

- 1 tbsp olive oil
- ½ large onion, chopped
- 2 bay leaves
- 120 g carrot grated
- 1 large red pepper chopped
- 215 g couscous Israeli
- ½ tsp garam masala
- 400 ml water
- 2 tsp salt or to taste
- 1 tbsp lemon juice
- Coriander to garnish

1. Move slider to AIR FRY/STOVETOP. Select SEAR/SAUTÉ and set to 3. Select START/STOP to begin preheating. Once hot, add the oil to the pot. 2. Add the onion and bay leaves. Sauté for 2 minutes. Add the carrots and pepper . Sauté for 1 minute more. Add the couscous, garam masala, water and salt. Stir well. 3. Close the lid and move slider to PRESSURE. Ensuring the pressure release valve is in the SEAL position. The temperature will default to HIGH, which is the correct setting. Set time to 2 minutes. Select START/STOP to begin cooking. 4. Once cooking is complete, use a Natural Release for 10 minutes, then release any remaining pressure. 5. Fluff the couscous and add the lemon juice. Garnish with coriander and serve warm.

Per Serving: Calories 106; Fat 2.91g; Sodium 952mg; Carbs 17.58g; Fibre 1.9g; Sugar 2.29g; Protein 2.69g

Rosemary Apricot Scones

Prep time: 25 minutes | **Cook time:** 15 minutes | **Serves:** 16

480 g plain flour
2 tbsp. sugar
2 tbsp. baking powder
¾ tsp. salt
340 g cold butter, cubed
Topping:
1 large egg, lightly beaten
2 tbsp. low fat milk

190 g chopped dried apricots
1 tbsp. minced fresh rosemary
4 large eggs, lightly beaten
240 g cold whipping cream

2 tsp. sugar

1. Combine flour, sugar, baking powder, and salt in a bowl. Add cold butter and mix until it resembles pea-sized pieces. Then, add apricots and rosemary and mix. 2. In a separate bowl, whisk together eggs and whipping cream. Combine the two mixtures until just moistened. 3. Turn onto a well-floured surface. Roll dough into a 25 cm square. Cut into four squares; cut each square into four triangles. Place on baking sheets lined with parchment paper. 4. For topping, combine egg and milk. Brush tops of scones with egg mixture; sprinkle with sugar. 5. Place the baking sheets on the bottom layer of the Deluxe Reversible Rack in the lower position. 6. When the pot has preheated, place the rack with pan in the pot. Close the lid and make sure the slider is in the AIR FRY/STOVETOP. 7. Select BAKE/ROAST, set temperature to 205°C, and set time to 15 minutes. Select START/STOP to begin cooking. Bake until golden brown, serve.
Per Serving: Calories 347; Fat 22.84g; Sodium 254mg; Carbs 31.3g; Fibre 1.8g; Sugar 6g; Protein 5g

Mushroom Congee Breakfast Bowl

Prep time: 10 minutes | **Cook time:** 20 minutes | **Serves:** 4-6

200 g uncooked jasmine rice
1.68 L water
100 g stemmed and sliced shiitake mushrooms
¼ tsp sesame oil
½ tsp dried minced garlic
½ tsp dried minced onion

½ tsp salt
3 large slices peeled fresh ginger
1 tsp everything bagel seasoning mix
Optional toppings: soft-boiled egg, sriracha sauce, soy sauce, sliced green onions

1. Mix together the rice, water, mushrooms, sesame oil, garlic, onion, salt and ginger and add to the pot. 2. Close the lid and move slider to PRESSURE. Ensuring the pressure release valve is in the SEAL position. The temperature will default to HIGH, which is the correct setting. Set time to 20 minutes. Select START/STOP to begin cooking. 3. When cooking is complete, release the pressure quickly by turning the pressure release valve to the VENT position. Move slider to the right to unlock the lid, then carefully open it. 4. Taste the congee and adjust the salt, if needed. 5. Place equal portions of congee in individual bowls. 6. Top each with ¼ to ½ teaspoon of everything bagel seasoning, plus an egg, sriracha, soy sauce and/or sliced green onions (if using).
Per Serving: Calories 120; Fat 7.35g; Sodium 330mg; Carbs 16g; Fibre 5.5g; Sugar 2.48g; Protein 4.98g

Garlic Cheese Bread

Prep time: 30 minutes | **Cook time:** 25 minutes | **Serves:** 2

1 pkg. (5g) active dry yeast
300 ml warm water
2 tbsp. plus 2 tsp. olive oil
7 garlic cloves, minced
1 tbsp. sugar
Egg Wash:
1 large egg

½ tsp. salt
1½ tsp. white vinegar
170 g – 200 g bread flour
100 g cubed Asiago cheese

1 tbsp. Water

1. In a large bowl, dissolve yeast in warm water. Add the oil, garlic, sugar, salt, vinegar and 150 g flour. Beat until smooth. Stir in enough of the remaining flour to form a firm dough. Stir in cheese. 2. Turn onto a floured surface; knead until smooth and elastic, 6-8 minutes. Place in a greased bowl, turning once to grease the top. Cover and let rise in a warm place until doubled, about 1 hour. 3. Punch dough down; divide in half. Shape into 12cm -round loaves. Place on lightly greased baking sheets. Cover and let rise in a warm place until doubled, about 30 minutes. 4. For egg wash, in a small bowl, combine egg and water. Brush over loaves. 5. Place the baking sheets on the bottom layer of the Deluxe Reversible Rack in the lower position. 6. When the pot has preheated, place the rack with pan in the pot. Close the lid and make sure the slider is in the AIR FRY/STOVETOP. Select BAKE/ROAST, set temperature to 190°C, and set time to 25 minutes. Select START/STOP to begin cooking. 7. When cooking is complete, remove the rack with the baking sheets and let cool for 5 minutes, then serve warm.
Per Serving: Calories 822; Fat 52.83g; Sodium 823mg; Carbs 24.83g; Fibre 1.8g; Sugar 7.45g; Protein 61g

Jalapeño–Cheddar Bagel Egg Casserole

Prep time: 10 minutes | **Cook time:** 20 minutes | **Serves:** 4

240 ml water
6 large eggs
60 g whipping cream
Salt
Freshly ground black pepper
1 jalapeño pepper, thinly sliced

1½ jalapeño-cheddar bagels, cut into 1 cm pieces
50 g shredded cheddar cheese
1 tbsp feta cheese crumbles
Unsalted butter, for baking dish
Chopped fresh coriander , for garnish

1. Pour the water into the pot of Ninja XL Pressure Cooker. 2. In a bowl, combine the eggs, cream, salt and black pepper to taste and the jalapeño and mix until the eggs are beaten. Stir in the bagel pieces and cheeses. Let sit for 3 minutes. 3. Butter a round baking dish that can fit the pot. Pour the egg mixture into the prepared baking dish. Place the pan on the bottom layer of the Deluxe Reversible Rack in the lower position. 4. Close the lid and move slider to PRESSURE. Ensuring the pressure release valve is in the SEAL position. The temperature will default to HIGH, which is the correct setting. Set time to 20 minutes. Select START/STOP to begin cooking. 5. When cooking is complete, release the pressure quickly by turning the pressure release valve to the VENT position. Move slider to the right to unlock the lid, then carefully open it. 6. Let the casserole cool for 5 minutes and then garnish with chopped fresh coriander.
Per Serving: Calories 336; Fat 21.32g; Sodium 1165mg; Carbs 22.44g; Fibre 1.8g; Sugar 4.96g; Protein 14g

Homemade Gingerbread French Toast Casserole

Prep time: 10 minutes | **Cook time:** 25 minutes | **Serves:** 4

2 tbsp unsalted butter	2 tbsp coconut sugar or dark brown sugar
½ loaf French bread or sourdough bread, cut into 2.5 cm chunks	1 tsp ground ginger
	1 tsp ground cinnamon
Nonstick cooking spray, for bowl or pan	¼ tsp ground cloves
3 large eggs	Pinch of salt
180 ml whole milk or nut milk	240 ml water
75 g molasses	Pure maple syrup, for serving

1. Move the slider to AIR FRY/STOVETOP, select SEAR/SAUTÉ and set temperature to 2. Once the pot is hot, add the butter and stir until melted, then add the bread cubes. Cook, tossing them around a bit, so all the bread cubes become lightly browned and toasty, 6 to 7 minutes. Press START/STOP to turn off the SEAR/SAUTÉ function. 2. Lightly spray a 15cm or 18 cm glass bowl with nonstick cooking spray. Place the bread cubes in the bowl and set aside. 3. In a separate bowl, whisk together the eggs, milk, ginger, cinnamon, molasses, coconut sugar, cloves and salt. Pour the egg mixture on top of the bread and gently toss. Cover the bowl with foil. 4. Pour the water into the pot. Place the casserole bowl on the bottom layer of the Deluxe Reversible Rack in the lower position in the pot. 5. Close the lid and move slider to PRESSURE. Ensuring the pressure release valve is in the SEAL position. The temperature will default to HIGH, which is the correct setting. Set time to 15 minutes. Select START/STOP to begin cooking. 6. When cooking is complete, release the pressure quickly by turning the pressure release valve to the VENT position. Move slider to the right to unlock the lid, then carefully open it. 7. Gently remove the bowl, using pot holders. Serve the casserole hot with warm maple syrup.

Per Serving: Calories 322; Fat 9.64g; Sodium 344mg; Carbs 53.91g; Fibre 1.1g; Sugar 39.67g; Protein 6g

Creamy Strawberry Oats

Prep time: 10 minutes | **Cook time:** 10 minutes | **Serves:** 2-4

480 ml water	160 ml whole milk
25 g rolled oats	1 pinch of salt
2 tbsp strawberries, freeze-dried (or your favourite dried or frozen fruit)	½ tsp white sugar (or to taste)

1. Add 480 ml of water to the pot of your Ninja XL Pressure Cooker and place the bottom layer of the Deluxe Reversible Rack in the lower position in the pot. 2. In a small-sized, heat-safe mug or bowl, add the oats, strawberries, milk, and salt. 3. Place the bowl on the rack. Close the lid and move slider to PRESSURE. Ensuring the pressure release valve is in the SEAL position. The temperature will default to HIGH, which is the correct setting. Set time to 10 minutes. Select START/STOP to begin cooking. 4. Close the lid and move the slider to PRESSURE, cook at HIGH pressure for 10 minutes. 5. When the cooking time is complete, use a Natural Release for 7-10 minutes, then release any remaining pressure. 6. Carefully remove the bowl from the pot. Mix the contents vigorously and then sprinkle with sugar to taste. Serve.

Per Serving: Calories 78; Fat 2.52g; Sodium 260mg; Carbs 14.56g; Fibre 1.8g; Sugar 7.59g; Protein 3.48g

Chapter 2 Soup, Chili and Stew Recipes

French Onion Cheese Soup

Prep time: 10 minutes | **Cook time:** 30 minutes | **Serves:** 4

1 tablespoon olive oil
1.2 kg medium yellow onions, halved and sliced through root end
1 tablespoon balsamic vinegar
4 medium garlic cloves, chopped
1 teaspoon chopped fresh thyme, or ½ teaspoon dried
120 ml dry sherry or vermouth
1.68 L Homemade Beef Stock
Salt and freshly ground black pepper
125 g aged Gruyère cheese, grated, rind reserved
½ loaf French baguette

1. Put the oil in the pot, move slider to AIR FRY/STOVETOP. Select SEAR/SAUTÉ and set to Hi 5. When the oil is hot, add half of the onions and cook, stirring often, until they begin to brown, 8 minutes. 2. Add the remaining onions and vinegar and continue to cook, stirring occasionally, until there is a deep brown glaze on the bottom of the pot, 4 minutes. 3. Add the garlic and thyme and cook until fragrant, 45 seconds. Add the vermouth and simmer for 1 minute, scraping up the browned residue from the base of the pot. Press START/STOP. 4. Add the stock, ½ teaspoon salt, and several grinds of pepper. Add the Gruyère rind to the pot. 5. Close the lid and move slider to PRESSURE, Ensuring the pressure release valve is in the SEAL position. The temperature will default to HIGH, which is the correct setting. Set time to 8 minutes. Select START/STOP to begin cooking. 6. When the cooking time is complete, release the pressure quickly by turning the pressure release valve to the VENT position. Move slider to the right to unlock the lid, then carefully open it. Discard the cheese rind and season the soup with salt and pepper. 7. Meanwhile, prepare the French baguette: Line a baking sheet with foil and adjust the oven rack so that it is 2 to 3 inches from the grilling element. 8. Cut the baguette at an angle into 2 cm-thick slices. Arrange the bread slices on the baking sheet. Carefully sprinkle 100 g of the grated cheese on the bread, and grill until the cheese is browned and bubbly, 3 minutes. 9. Ladle the soup into large soup bowls, top with the cheese toasts, and sprinkle the remaining cheese over the top. Serve.

Per Serving: Calories 753; Fat 45.52g; Sodium 1220mg; Carbs 75.27g; Fibre 6.9g; Sugar 23g; Protein 12.24g

Salmon, Leek, and Potato Soup

Prep time: 10 minutes | **Cook time:** 15 minutes | **Serves:** 6

455 g leeks (3 large)
2 tablespoons butter
960 ml store-bought chicken or vegetable stock, or homemade
3 large russet potatoes, peeled and cut into 5 cm chunks
2 bay leaves
Salt and freshly ground black pepper
120 g whipping cream
250 g hot-smoked wild salmon, skin and bones discarded, at room temperature

1. Trim the toughest green part and root end from the leeks and discard. Halve the leeks lengthwise, rinse thoroughly under cold water to remove grit between the layers, and chop. 2. Add the butter to the pot, move slider to AIR FRY/STOVETOP. Select SEAR/SAUTÉ and set to 3. Open lid and select START/STOP to begin cooking. 3. When the butter has melted, add the leeks. Cover with a regular pot lid and sauté, stirring occasionally, until the leeks are tender, 4 minutes. (The lid traps steam, melting the leeks without browning them.) Press START/STOP. 4. Add the stock, bay leaves, potatoes, and ½ teaspoon salt and stir to combine. 5. Close the lid and move slider to PRESSURE function. Ensuring the pressure release valve is in the SEAL position. The temperature will default to HIGH, which is the correct setting. Set time to 10 minutes. Select START/STOP to begin cooking. 6. When cooking is complete, release the pressure quickly by turning the pressure release valve to the VENT position. Move slider to the right to unlock the lid, then carefully open it. Using an immersion blender, blend the soup in the pot until mostly smooth. 7. Alternatively, blend the soup in batches in a standing blender with the lid slightly ajar and a towel draped over the lid to prevent splatters. Season with salt and pepper, keeping in mind that the salmon is salty. 8. Divide the soup among six bowls. Flake the salmon and place small mounds of it on top of each bowl of soup.

Per Serving: Calories 430; Fat 16.37g; Sodium 801mg; Carbs 51.92g; Fibre 4.7g; Sugar 8.06g; Protein 20.83g

Corned Beef and Beans Chili

Prep time: 10 minutes | **Cook time:** 30 minutes | **Serves:** 6

One can diced tomatoes, preferably fire-roasted
One 360 ml bottle Guinness stout
2 tablespoons pure chili powder
2 tablespoons mild smoked paprika
1 teaspoon ground cumin
1 teaspoon dried oregano
1 medium yellow onion, chopped
900 g low-sodium raw corned beef, rinsed and any spice packets removed, the meat diced
Two cans pink beans, drained and rinsed

1. Add the tomatoes, Guinness, cumin, chili powder, smoked paprika, oregano, onion, and corned beef to the pot and stir well. Close the lid and move slider to PRESSURE. Ensuring the pressure release valve is in the SEAL position. The temperature will default to HIGH, which is the correct setting. Set time to 22 minutes. Select START/STOP to begin cooking. 2. When cooking is complete, release the pressure quickly by turning the pressure release valve to the VENT position. Move slider to the right to unlock the lid, then carefully open it. Stir in the beans. 3. Lock the lid back onto the pot. Move slider to PRESSURE function and cook on high for 8 minutes. Stir well before serving.

Per Serving: Calories 301; Fat 4.59g; Sodium 107mg; Carbs 55.29g; Fibre 7.1g; Sugar 18.48g; Protein 14.83g

Thai-Style Butternut Bisque

Prep time: 10 minutes | **Cook time:** 20 minutes | **Serves:** 2-4

360 ml canned coconut milk (do not shake the can before opening)
1 tablespoon rapeseed oil
1 medium yellow onion, chopped
1 tablespoon red curry paste
1 medium butternut squash, seeded, peeled, and cut into large (4 cm) chunks
240 ml store-bought chicken or vegetable stock, or homemade
1 tablespoon fish sauce or soy sauce, plus more to taste
Salt and freshly ground black pepper

Optional Garnishes:
10 g fresh coriander leaves, chopped
30 g roasted unsalted peanuts, chopped

1. Set aside 2 tablespoons of the thick coconut milk from the top of the can for garnishing the soup. 2. Add oil to the pot. Move slider to AIR FRY/STOVETOP. Select SEAR/SAUTÉ and set to 3. Select START/STOP to begin preheating. Add the onion when the oil is hot. Cook and stir often, until beginning to brown, 6 minutes. Add the curry paste and cook, stirring frequently, until fragrant, 20 seconds. Press START/STOP. 3. Add the squash, remaining coconut milk, the stock, and the fish sauce. Lock on the lid, select the PRESSURE function, Ensuring the pressure release valve is in the SEAL position. The temperature will default to HIGH, which is the correct setting. Set time to 10 minutes. Select START/STOP to begin cooking. 4. When the cooking time is up, quick-release the pressure. 5. Blend the soup with an immersion blender or in batches in a standing blender with the lid slightly ajar and a towel over the top to prevent splatters. 6. Season the soup with more fish sauce, salt, and pepper. 7. Garnish with swirls of the reserved coconut milk and the optional garnishes, if desired.

Per Serving: Calories 541; Fat 48g; Sodium 581mg; Carbs 24.63g; Fibre 6.9g; Sugar 12.24g; Protein 11.31g

Creamy Cheese Chicken Soup

Prep time: 20 minutes | **Cook time:** 15 minutes | **Serves:** 6

4 tablespoons salted butter
1 medium onion, peeled and chopped
1 small jalapeño pepper, seeded and chopped
2 cloves garlic, peeled and minced
1 tablespoon chili powder
½ teaspoon salt
½ teaspoon ground black pepper
3 tablespoons flour
720 ml chicken stock
1 (250 g) can diced tomatoes with green chilies
420 g shredded cooked chicken breast
120 g heavy whipping cream
200 g shredded Cheddar cheese
10 g chopped fresh coriander
3 ounces tortilla chips

1. Move slider to AIR FRY/STOVETOP. Select SEAR/SAUTÉ and set to 3. Select START/STOP to begin preheating. Heat the butter until melted. 2. Then add onion, jalapeño, and garlic and cook until tender, about 8 minutes. Add chili powder, salt, and pepper and cook until fragrant, about 30 seconds. 3. Sprinkle flour over vegetables and cook, stirring well, until flour is completely moistened, about 1 minute. 4. Slowly whisk in stock, making sure to scrape any bits off the bottom of the pot. Press the START/STOP button and stir in tomatoes and chicken. Close the lid and move slider to PRESSURE. Ensuring the pressure release valve is in the SEAL position. The temperature will default to HIGH, which is the correct setting. Set time to 5 minutes. Select START/STOP to begin cooking. 5. When cooking is complete, release the pressure quickly by turning the pressure release valve to the VENT position. Move slider to the right to unlock the lid, then carefully open it. 6. Stir the soup well, then stir in cream. Add cheese 50 g at a time, allowing the first addition to melt before adding the next. Serve hot with coriander and tortilla chips for garnish.

Per Serving: Calories 299; Fat 13.52g; Sodium 1198mg; Carbs 17.68g; Fibre 1.4g; Sugar 3.42g; Protein 26.58g

Beef and Sausage Soup with Pepperoni

Prep time: 20 minutes | **Cook time:** 20 minutes | **Serves:** 8

225 g Italian sausage	½ teaspoon ground fennel
225 g 80% lean beef mince	1 (700 g) jar marinara sauce
1 medium onion, peeled and diced	1 can crushed tomatoes
1 medium green pepper , seeded and chopped	240 ml water
1 medium red pepper , seeded and chopped	120 g shredded mozzarella cheese
2 cloves garlic, peeled and minced	70 g sliced black olives
1 teaspoon Italian seasoning	55 g mini pepperoni slices

1. Add sausage and beef to the pot. Move slider to AIR FRY/STOVETOP. Select SEAR/SAUTÉ and set to Lo1. Select START/STOP to begin cooking. 2. Cook, crumbling, until browned, about 8 minutes. 3. Add onion and peppers and cook until tender, about 6 minutes, then add garlic, Italian seasoning, and fennel and cook for 30 seconds. Press START/STOP to turn off the SEAR/SAUTÉ function. 4. Add marinara sauce, tomatoes, and water. Close the lid and move slider to PRESSURE. Ensuring the pressure release valve is in the SEAL position. The temperature will default to HIGH, which is the correct setting. Set time to 10 minutes. Select START/STOP to begin cooking. 5. When cooking is complete, release the pressure quickly by turning the pressure release valve to the VENT position. Move slider to the right to unlock the lid, then carefully open it. 6. Ladle into bowls and top with mozzarella, olives, and pepperoni.

Per Serving: Calories 207; Fat 8.76g; Sodium 1169mg; Carbs 15.14g; Fibre 4.6g; Sugar 7.09g; Protein 19.77g

Beans and Kale Soup

Prep time: 15 minutes | **Cook time:** 13 minutes | **Serves:** 2

½ tablespoon oil	150 g diced tomatoes with their juices
½ onion, chopped	¼ teaspoon red pepper flakes
1 medium carrot, thickly sliced	1 small Parmesan chunk with rind, plus shaved Parmesan cheese for garnish
1 garlic clove, finely chopped	Salt
1 thyme sprig	Freshly ground black pepper
1 can cannellini beans, drained and rinsed	60 g chopped kale
600 ml vegetable stock or water	

1. Move slider to AIR FRY/STOVETOP. Select SEAR/SAUTÉ and set to 3. Select START/STOP to begin preheating. Heat the oil and add the onion and carrot and cook until softened, 4 to 5 minutes. Add the garlic and cook until fragrant, 1 minute. 2. Add the thyme, beans, stock, tomatoes and their juices, red pepper flakes, and Parmesan rind. Season with salt and pepper. Press START/STOP to turn off the SEAR/SAUTÉ function. 3. Close the lid and move slider to PRESSURE. Ensuring the pressure release valve is in the SEAL position. The temperature will default to HIGH, which is the correct setting. Set time to 8 minutes. Select START/STOP to begin cooking. 4. When cooking is complete, naturally release the pressure for 10 minutes. Then release the pressure quickly by turning the pressure release valve to the VENT position. Move slider to AIR FRY/ STOVETOP to unlock the lid, then carefully open it. 5. Remove the thyme stem and the Parmesan rind and stir in the kale. Taste and season with salt and pepper as desired. 6. Serve garnished with shaved Parmesan cheese.

Per Serving: Calories 162; Fat 5.38g; Sodium 954mg; Carbs 22.1g; Fibre 4.8g; Sugar 6.41g; Protein 9.7g

Cheddar Broccoli and Potato Soup

Prep time: 10 minutes | **Cook time:** 15 minutes | **Serves:** 4

1 tablespoon olive oil
1 medium yellow onion, chopped
455 g broccoli crowns, florets left in 8 cm pieces, stems sliced
480 ml store-bought vegetable or chicken stock, or homemade
1 large russet potato, peeled and chopped
Salt and freshly ground black pepper
120 g whipping cream, warmed
50 g grated aged cheddar cheese
½ to ¾ teaspoon freshly grated nutmeg

1. Put the oil in the pot, move slider to AIR FRY/STOVETOP. Select SEAR/SAUTÉ and set to 3. Select START/STOP to begin preheating. When the oil is hot, add the onion and cook, stirring often, until beginning to brown, 4 minutes. Press START/STOP. 2. Add the broccoli, potatoes, stock, ½ teaspoon salt, and a few grinds of pepper and stir to combine. 3. Close the lid and move slider to PRESSURE function, Ensuring the pressure release valve is in the SEAL position. The temperature will default to HIGH, which is the correct setting. Set time to 10 minutes. Select START/STOP to begin cooking. 4. When the cooking time is up, let the pressure come down naturally for 10 minutes and then quick-release the remaining pressure. 5. Add the cream and cheese and whisk to combine and break up the vegetables. 6. Season the soup with the nutmeg and additional salt and pepper.

Per Serving: Calories 288; Fat 14.4g; Sodium 859mg; Carbs 32.08g; Fibre 5.6g; Sugar 6.43g; Protein 10.93g

Spiced Yellow Lentil and Spinach Soup

Prep time: 10 minutes | **Cook time:** 30 minutes | **Serves:** 6

2 tablespoons olive oil
2 stalks celery, sliced
1 medium yellow onion, peeled and roughly chopped
1 medium carrot, peeled and sliced
2 cloves garlic, peeled and minced
1 teaspoon fresh minced ginger
½ teaspoon ground cumin
½ teaspoon ground turmeric
¼ teaspoon smoked paprika
½ teaspoon salt
400 g dried yellow lentils
960 ml roasted vegetable stock
120 g baby spinach
1 tablespoon lemon juice

1. Add oil to the pot. Move slider to AIR FRY/STOVETOP. Select SEAR/SAUTÉ and set to 3. Select START/STOP to begin preheating. 2. Once the oil is hot, add celery, onion, and carrot and cook until just tender, about 3 minutes. Add garlic, ginger, cumin, turmeric, paprika, and salt. Cook until fragrant, about 1 minute. Press the START/STOP button. 3. Add lentils and stock to pot. Close the lid and move slider to PRESSURE, Ensuring the pressure release valve is in the SEAL position. The temperature will default to HIGH, which is the correct setting. Set time to 25 minutes. Select START/STOP to begin cooking. 4. When the time is up, let pressure release naturally, about 15 minutes. Remove lid and stir in spinach and lemon juice. Close lid and let stand for 10 minutes. Serve warm.

Per Serving: Calories 143; Fat 6.18g; Sodium 596mg; Carbs 18.94g; Fibre 3.2g; Sugar 3.39g; Protein 6.11g

Creamy Cheese Tomato Basil Soup

Prep time: 10 minutes | **Cook time:** 10 minutes | **Serves:** 4

2 tablespoons olive oil (or the oil from the sun-dried tomato jar)	45 g chopped drained oil-packed sun-dried tomatoes
1 medium yellow onion, chopped	1 tablespoon sherry vinegar
1 can San Marzano–style whole tomatoes, with their juice, roughly chopped	50 g grated Parmigiano Reggiano cheese
	120 g whipping cream
480 ml store-bought chicken or vegetable stock, or homemade	Salt and freshly ground black pepper
	30 g fresh basil leaves, stacked, rolled into a tight cylinder, and thinly sliced crosswise into ribbons

1. Put the oil in the pot, move slider to AIR FRY/STOVETOP. Select SEAR/SAUTÉ and set to 3. Select START/STOP to begin preheating. When the oil is hot, add the onion and cook, stirring often, until tender, 4 minutes. Press START/STOP. 2. Add the tomatoes and juice, sun-dried tomatoes, stock, and vinegar. Close the lid and move slider to PRESSURE, Ensuring the pressure release valve is in the SEAL position. The temperature will default to HIGH, which is the correct setting. Set time to 5 minutes. Select START/STOP to begin cooking. 3. When cooking is complete, release the pressure quickly by turning the pressure release valve to the VENT position. Move slider to the right to unlock the lid, then carefully open it. 4. Use an immersion blender to blend the soup until smooth. Alternatively, in a blender with the lid slightly ajar, blend the soup in batches. Drape a towel over the lid to prevent splatters. Return the soup to the pot. 5. Add the cheese and cream and stir to combine. Season with salt and pepper. Serve garnished with the basil.
Per Serving: Calories 308; Fat 20.44g; Sodium 995mg; Carbs 23.61g; Fibre 3.4g; Sugar 12.47g; Protein 8.61g

Chili Beef Hot Dog Soup

Prep time: 20 minutes | **Cook time:** 30 minutes | **Serves:** 8

455 g 80% lean beef mince	½ teaspoon salt
1 medium white onion, peeled and chopped	½ teaspoon ground black pepper
2 cloves garlic, peeled and minced	1 can diced tomatoes
10 g chili powder	48 ml Beef Stock
1 teaspoon ground cumin	8 all-beef hot dogs, chopped
½ teaspoon ground coriander	100 g shredded Cheddar cheese
2 tablespoons light brown sugar	70 g finely chopped Vidalia onion

1. Move slider to AIR FRY/STOVETOP. Select SEAR/SAUTÉ and set to 3. Select START/STOP to begin preheating. Brown the beef mince until no pink remains, about 10 minutes. Add white onion, garlic, coriander, chili powder, cumin, brown sugar, salt, and pepper and cook until the onions are just tender, about 10 minutes. 2. Add tomatoes, stock, and hot dogs and stir well. Press START/STOP to turn off the SEAR/SAUTÉ function. Close the lid and move slider to PRESSURE. Ensuring the pressure release valve is in the SEAL position. The temperature will default to HIGH, which is the correct setting. Set time to 20 minutes. Select START/STOP to begin cooking. 3. When cooking is complete, naturally release the pressure for 20 minutes. Then release the pressure quickly by turning the pressure release valve to the VENT position. Move slider to AIR FRY/ STOVETOP to unlock the lid, then carefully open it, stir well. 4. Serve hot with cheese and Vidalia onion for garnish.
Per Serving: Calories 287; Fat 8.02g; Sodium 1148mg; Carbs 38.4g; Fibre 4.7g; Sugar 5.62g; Protein 19.93g

Pearled Barley–Lentil Soup with Spinach

Prep time: 20 minutes | **Cook time:** 6 hours 20 minutes | **Serves:** 4

2 tablespoons extra-virgin olive oil, plus more to serve
1 medium yellow onion, chopped
6 medium garlic cloves, finely chopped
2 medium carrots, peeled, quartered lengthwise and sliced 1 cm thick
2 tablespoons tomato paste
4 bay leaves
Salt and ground black pepper
1 tablespoon grated lime zest, plus 3 tablespoons lime juice, plus lime wedges to serve
160 g pearled barley
100 g brown or green lentils
1.5 L low-sodium vegetable stock
75 g lightly packed baby spinach, chopped
35 g lightly packed fresh coriander, chopped

1. Move slider to AIR FRY/STOVETOP. Select SEAR/SAUTÉ and set to Hi 5. Select START/STOP to begin preheating. 2. Add the oil and heat until shimmering. Add the onion, garlic, carrots, tomato paste, bay leaves and 1 teaspoon salt. Cook and stir occasionally, until the vegetables begin to brown, about 5 minutes. Stir in the lime zest and juice, lentils, barley and stock, scraping up any browned bits, then distribute in an even layer. Press START/STOP. 3. Close the lid and move slider to PRESSURE. Ensuring the pressure release valve is in the SEAL position. The temperature will default to HIGH, which is the correct setting. Set time to 15 minutes. Select START/STOP to begin cooking. 4. When cooking is complete, release the pressure quickly by turning the pressure release valve to the VENT position. Move slider to the right to unlock the lid, then carefully open it. 5. With the pot still on SEAR/SAUTÉ function, bring the mixture to a boil. Press START/STOP. 6. Lock the lid in place and move the pressure valve to Vent. Select Slow Cook and set the temperature to Lo. Set the cooking time for 6 hours; the soup is done when the barley and lentils are fully tender. Press START/STOP, then carefully open the pot. 7. Remove and discard the bay, then stir in the spinach and coriander. Taste and season with salt and pepper. 8. Serve drizzled with oil and with lime wedges on the side.
Per Serving: Calories 396; Fat 5.71g; Sodium 962mg; Carbs 74.66g; Fibre 17.5g; Sugar 12.12g; Protein 19.73g

Spicy Black Bean Soup

Prep time: 10 minutes | **Cook time:** 8 minutes | **Serves:** 4

690 g drained Simple Black Beans, plus 720 ml cooking liquid
1 chipotle chili in adobo, minced
20 g finely chopped fresh coriander
2 tablespoons lime juice
Salt and ground black pepper

1. In a large saucepan over medium, combine the beans, the 720 ml cooking liquid and the chipotle chili. Cook, stirring often, until heated through, 5 to 8 minutes. 2. Off heat, stir in the coriander and lime juice. Taste and season with salt and pepper.
Per Serving: Calories 236; Fat 1.06g; Sodium 23mg; Carbs 43.89g; Fibre 15.5g; Sugar 0.77g; Protein 15.63g

Thai Spiced Lentil and Coconut Milk Soup

Prep time: 10 minutes | **Cook time:** 25 minutes | **Serves:** 6

2 tablespoons olive oil
2 stalks celery, sliced
1 medium white onion, peeled and chopped
2 medium carrots, peeled and sliced
2 cloves garlic, minced
1 teaspoon minced ginger
1 tablespoon Thai red curry paste
½ teaspoon ground coriander
½ teaspoon ground cumin
¼ teaspoon cayenne pepper
¼ teaspoon smoked paprika
½ teaspoon salt
400 g dried green lentils
1 large russet potato, peeled and cubed
960 ml Roasted Vegetable Stock
1 can full-fat coconut milk
2 tablespoons fresh lime juice
2 tablespoons chopped fresh coriander
½ teaspoon black pepper

1. Move slider to AIR FRY/STOVETOP. Select SEAR/SAUTÉ and set to 3. Select START/STOP to begin preheating. 2. Heat the oil and add celery, onion, and carrots and cook until just tender, about 3 minutes. 3. Add garlic, ginger, cumin, curry paste, coriander, cayenne pepper, paprika, and salt. Cook until fragrant, about 30 seconds. Press the START/STOP button. 4. Add lentils, stock, potato, and coconut milk to pot and stir well. 5. Close the lid, move slider to PRESSURE. Ensuring the pressure release valve is in the SEAL position. The temperature will default to HIGH, which is the correct setting. Set time to 20 minutes. Select START/STOP to begin cooking. 6. When the time is up, let pressure release naturally, about 15 minutes. Remove lid and stir in lime juice. 7. Serve warm with coriander and black pepper for garnish.
Per Serving: Calories 349; Fat 22.6g; Sodium 595mg; Carbs 34.05g; Fibre 5.7g; Sugar 6.05g; Protein 8.6g

Pepperoni, Cheese Ravioli and Mushroom Pizza Stew

Prep time: 15 minutes | **Cook time:** 15 minutes | **Serves:** 6

2 tablespoons vegetable oil
1 medium onion, peeled and chopped
200 g sliced button mushrooms
1 green pepper, seeded and chopped
2 cloves garlic, peeled and minced
1 tablespoon Italian seasoning
2 cans diced tomatoes
480 ml Beef Stock
115 g sliced pepperoni
1 (225 g) package refrigerated cheese ravioli
120 g shredded mozzarella cheese

1. Move slider to AIR FRY/STOVETOP. Select SEAR/SAUTÉ and set to Lo1. Select START/STOP to begin preheating. Heat the oil and add onion, mushrooms, and pepper and cook until vegetables are tender, about 8 minutes. Add garlic and Italian seasoning and cook until fragrant, about 30 seconds. 2. Add tomatoes, stock, and pepperoni to pot and stir well. Press START/STOP to turn off the SEAR/SAUTÉ function. Close the lid and move slider to PRESSURE. Ensuring the pressure release valve is in the SEAL position. The temperature will default to HIGH, which is the correct setting. Set time to 5 minutes. Select START/STOP to begin cooking. 3. When the time is up, release the pressure quickly by turning the pressure release valve to the VENT position. Move slider to the right to unlock the lid, then carefully open it. Stir in ravioli, close lid, cook on PRESSURE function for additional 1 minute. 4. When the timer beeps, quick-release the pressure, open lid, and stir soup. Serve hot with shredded cheese for garnish.
Per Serving: Calories 245; Fat 13.89g; Sodium 1042mg; Carbs 16.49g; Fibre 4.3g; Sugar 7.46g; Protein 14.69g

Beef Brisket & Butternut Squash Chili

Prep time: 10 minutes | **Cook time:** 45 minutes | **Serves:** 4

8 dried chilis, preferably new mexico red, passila, ancho, and/or mulato chilis, stemmed and seeded	1 tablespoon cumin seeds
½ small red onion, roughly chopped	1 tablespoon dried oregano
1 canned chipotle in adobo sauce, stemmed and seeded	1 teaspoon table salt
2 medium garlic cloves, peeled	2 tablespoons olive oil
1½ tablespoons red wine vinegar	900 g boneless beef brisket, diced
1½ tablespoons honey	One 360 ml bottle of beer, preferably an amber ale or a pilsner (gluten-free, if necessary)
1 tablespoon adobo sauce from the can	455 g peeled butternut squash cubes, about 2.5 cm pieces

1. Bring a big saucepan of water to a boil over high heat. Turn off the heat, add the chilis, cover the pan, and soak for 20 minutes. Or do this whole operation in the Ninja XL Pressure Cooker. 2. Move slider to AIR FRY/STOVETOP. Select SEAR/SAUTÉ and set to Hi 5, press START/STOP to begin cooking, heat the water until boiled. Add the chilis and soak for 20 minutes. Press START/STOP. 3. Drain the chilis in a colander set in the sink and pile them into a large blender. Add the onion, chipotle, garlic, vinegar, honey, adobo sauce, cumin, oregano, and salt. Cover and blend into a coarse paste, stopping the machine at least once to scrape down the inside. 4. Select SEAR/SAUTÉ and set to 3. Heat the oil in the for a couple of minutes, then add every speck of the chili paste from the blender. Cook for 2 minutes, stirring often, to toast the paste. 5. Add the brisket and stir well to get every little bit coated in the paste. Pour in the beer and stir well. 6. Press the START/STOP to turn off the SEAR/SAUTÉ function. Close the lid and move slider to PRESSURE. Ensuring the pressure release valve is in the SEAL position. The temperature will default to HIGH, which is the correct setting. Set time to 25 minutes. Select START/STOP to begin cooking. 7. When cooking is complete, release the pressure quickly by turning the pressure release valve to the VENT position. Move slider to the right to unlock the lid, then carefully open it. 8. Stir in the butternut squash cubes. Lock the lid back onto the pot. move slider to PRESSURE. Cook on high temp for 3 minutes. 9. Stir well before serving.

Per Serving: Calories 820; Fat 5.61g; Sodium 1194mg; Carbs 38.66g; Fibre 5.9g; Sugar 16.78g; Protein 42.67g

Cumin Bacon and Black Bean Chili

Prep time: 10 minutes | **Cook time:** 20 minutes | **Serves:** 4

1 tablespoon butter	1 can black beans, drained and rinsed
455 g thick-cut or slab bacon (not pepper bacon or other flavoured bacon), chopped	2½ tablespoons pure chili powder
1 medium yellow onion, chopped	2 teaspoons ground cumin
180 ml amber beer or chicken stock	2 medium garlic cloves, peeled and minced (2 teaspoons)
1 can diced tomatoes	2 canned chipotles in adobo sauce, stemmed, seeded, and chopped

1. Add butter to the pot. Move slider to AIR FRY/STOVETOP. Select SEAR/SAUTÉ and set to 3. Select START/STOP to begin preheating. 2. Once the butter is melted, add the bacon and onion. Cook, stirring frequently, until the bacon begins to brown well, about 8 minutes. Stir in the beer. Scrape up every speck of browned stuff on the pot's bottom. 3. Press START/STOP to turn off the SEAR/SAUTÉ function. Stir in the tomatoes, black beans, cumin, chili powder, garlic, and canned chipotles. Close the lid and move slider to PRESSURE. 4. Ensuring the pressure release valve is in the SEAL position. The temperature will default to HIGH, which is the correct setting. Set time to 8 minutes. Select START/STOP to begin cooking. 5. When cooking is complete, release the pressure quickly by turning the pressure release valve to the VENT position. Move slider to the right to unlock the lid, then carefully open it. Stir well before serving.

Per Serving: Calories 622; Fat 24.36g; Sodium 1030mg; Carbs 48g; Fibre 13.6g; Sugar 16.1g; Protein 53.21g

Yellow Lentil Soup

Prep time: 10 minutes | **Cook time:** 25 minutes | **Serves:** 6

2 tablespoons olive oil	½ teaspoon ground cumin
1 stalk celery, sliced	½ teaspoon salt
1 medium white onion, peeled and roughly chopped	400 g dried yellow lentils
1 medium carrot, peeled and sliced	1 large russet potato, peeled and chopped
2 cloves garlic, peeled and minced	960 ml beef stock or chicken stock
½ teaspoon ground turmeric	1 tablespoon fresh lemon juice

1. Move slider to AIR FRY/STOVETOP. Select SEAR/SAUTÉ and set to 3. Select START/STOP to begin preheating. 2. Heat the oil, add celery, onion, and carrot and cook until just tender, about 3 minutes. Add garlic, turmeric, cumin, and salt. Cook until fragrant, about 30 seconds. Press START/STOP to turn off the SEAR/SAUTÉ function. 3. Add lentils, potato, and stock to pot and stir well. Close the lid and move slider to PRESSURE. 4. Ensuring the pressure release valve is in the SEAL position. The temperature will default to HIGH, which is the correct setting. Set time to 20 minutes. Select START/STOP to begin cooking. 5. When cooking is complete, naturally release the pressure for 15 minutes. Then release the pressure quickly by turning the pressure release valve to the VENT position. Move slider to AIR FRY/ STOVETOP to unlock the lid, then carefully open it. 6. Stir in lemon juice. Purée soup with an immersion blender, or in batches in a blender, until smooth. Serve warm.

Per Serving: Calories 276; Fat 11.19g; Sodium 1274mg; Carbs 38.39g; Fibre 3.2g; Sugar 1.96g; Protein 9.1g

Spiced Red Lentil and Pumpkin Soup

Prep time: 10 minutes | **Cook time:** 25 minutes | **Serves:** 6

- 2 tablespoons olive oil
- 2 stalks celery, sliced
- 1 medium yellow onion, peeled and chopped
- 1 medium carrot, peeled and sliced
- 2 cloves garlic, peeled and minced
- 1 teaspoon minced fresh ginger
- ½ teaspoon ground coriander
- ½ teaspoon ground turmeric
- ¼ teaspoon ground allspice
- ¼ teaspoon ground cinnamon
- ⅛ teaspoon ground nutmeg
- ½ teaspoon salt
- 400 g dried red lentils
- 1 can pumpkin purée
- 720 ml roasted vegetable stock

1. Move slider to AIR FRY/STOVETOP. Select SEAR/SAUTÉ and set to 3. Select START/STOP to begin preheating. 2. Heat the oil, add celery, onion, and carrot and cook until just tender, about 3 minutes. Add garlic, ginger, cinnamon, coriander, turmeric, allspice, nutmeg, and salt. Cook until fragrant, about 30 seconds. Press START/STOP to turn off the SEAR/SAUTÉ function. 3. Add lentils, pumpkin, and stock to pot and stir well. Close the lid and move slider to PRESSURE. Ensuring the pressure release valve is in the SEAL position. The temperature will default to HIGH, which is the correct setting. Set time to 20 minutes. Select START/STOP to begin cooking. 4. When cooking is complete, release the pressure quickly by turning the pressure release valve to the VENT position. Move slider to the right to unlock the lid, then carefully open it. 5. When cooking is complete, naturally release the pressure for 15 minutes. Then release the pressure quickly by turning the pressure release valve to the VENT position. Move slider to AIR FRY/ STOVETOP to unlock the lid, then carefully open it and stir well. Serve warm.

Per Serving: Calories 414; Fat 10.86g; Sodium 491mg; Carbs 61.1g; Fibre 12.6g; Sugar 2.65g; Protein 21.49g

Loaded Vegetable and Green Lentil Stew

Prep time: 5 minutes | **Cook time:** 20 minutes | **Serves:** 6

- 2 tablespoons olive oil
- 2 stalks celery, sliced
- 2 medium carrots, peeled and sliced
- 1 medium yellow onion, peeled and chopped
- 2 cloves garlic, minced
- ½ teaspoon dried oregano
- ¼ teaspoon ground fennel
- ½ teaspoon salt
- 385 g green lentils
- 1 medium sweet potato, peeled and diced
- 1 can diced tomatoes, drained
- 960 ml roasted vegetable stock

1. Move slider to AIR FRY/STOVETOP. Select SEAR/SAUTÉ and set to 3. Select START/STOP to begin preheating. Heat the oil and add celery, carrots, and onion and cook until just tender, about 3 minutes. Add garlic, oregano, fennel, and salt. Cook until fragrant, about 30 seconds. Press START/STOP to turn off the SEAR/SAUTÉ function. 2. Add lentils, sweet potato, tomatoes, and stock. Close the lid and move slider to PRESSURE. 3. Ensuring the pressure release valve is in the SEAL position. The temperature will default to HIGH, which is the correct setting. Set time to 25 minutes. Select START/STOP to begin cooking. 4. When cooking is complete, naturally release the pressure for 15 minutes. Then release the pressure quickly by turning the pressure release valve to the VENT position. Move slider to AIR FRY/ STOVETOP to unlock the lid, then carefully open it. 5. Stir well and serve warm.

Per Serving: Calories 164; Fat 5.67g; Sodium 623mg; Carbs 25.37g; Fibre 4.8g; Sugar 7.9g; Protein 5.43g

Lamb and Carrot Stew

Prep time: 10 minutes | **Cook time:** 40 minutes | **Serves:** 4

2 tablespoons olive oil
900 g boneless leg of lamb, fat trimmed, cut into 2.5 cmpieces
Salt and freshly ground black pepper
1 medium yellow onion, thinly sliced through the root end
120 ml Guinness or Murphy's Irish stout
360 ml store-bought beef stock , or homemade
3 medium carrots, peeled and cut into 2.5 cm-thick coins
1 large russet potato, peeled and cut into 1 cm slices
2 tablespoons cornflour

1. Put the oil in the pot, move slider to AIR FRY/STOVETOP. Select SEAR/SAUTÉ and set to Hi 5. Select START/STOP to begin preheating. 2. Season the lamb all over with salt and pepper. Add 140 g of the meat (or the chops, in batches) to the pot and cook, stirring occasionally, until browned, 8 minutes. Do not overcrowd the meat or it will simmer in its juices instead of browning. 3. Add the onion to the pot, cook and stir occasionally, until the onion begins to brown, 5 minutes. Add the stout and cook for 1 minute, scraping up the browned bits on the bottom of the pot. Press START/STOP to turn off the SEAR/SAUTÉ function. 4. Add the remaining lamb, the stock , and the carrots and stir to combine. Place the potatoes on the top, but don't stir them into the lamb mixture. 5. Close the lid and move slider to PRESSURE, Ensuring the pressure release valve is in the SEAL position. The temperature will default to HIGH, which is the correct setting. Set time to 25 minutes. Select START/STOP to begin cooking. When the cooking time is up, let the pressure come down naturally for 10 minutes and then quick-release the remaining pressure. 6. Select SEAR/SAUTÉ and set to Hi 5. 7. Mix the cornflour with 2 tablespoons water and gently stir the mixture into the stew. Simmer until bubbly, 1 minute. Season with salt and pepper. Serve.
Per Serving: Calories 517; Fat 19.83g; Sodium 921mg; Carbs 33.53g; Fibre 2.6g; Sugar 2.84g; Protein 49.49g

Sweet Potato Lentil Soup with Spinach

Prep time: 10 minutes | **Cook time:** 18 minutes | **Serves:** 2

2 teaspoons oil
70 g diced yellow onion
60 g diced celery
60 g chopped carrot
1 large sweet potato, peeled and cubed
4 garlic cloves, minced
1 teaspoon ground cumin
1 teaspoon ground turmeric
½ teaspoon herbes de Provence
Salt
Freshly ground black pepper
150 g dry lentils
50 g dry split peas (or more lentils)
960 ml Vegetable Stock
15 g baby spinach
1 teaspoon red wine vinegar

1. Move slider to AIR FRY/STOVETOP. Select SEAR/SAUTÉ and set to 3. Select START/STOP to begin preheating. Heat the oil and add the onion, celery, carrot, and sweet potato and sauté until the vegetables begin to soften, about 5 minutes. 2. Stir in the garlic, cumin, turmeric, and herbes de Provence and cook for an additional 1 minute. Season with salt and pepper. Add the lentils, split peas, and stock. Stir together. Press START/STOP to turn off the SEAR/SAUTÉ function. 3. Close the lid and move slider to PRESSURE. Ensuring the pressure release valve is in the SEAL position. The temperature will default to HIGH, which is the correct setting. Set time to 12 minutes. Select START/STOP to begin cooking. 4. When cooking is complete, release the pressure quickly by turning the pressure release valve to the VENT position. Move slider to the right to unlock the lid, then carefully open it. 5. Stir in the spinach and vinegar and season with salt and pepper.
Per Serving: Calories 507; Fat 16.78g; Sodium 1012mg; Carbs 74.47g; Fibre 17g; Sugar 18.4g; Protein 19.32g

Beef and Mushroom Stroganoff Soup

Prep time: 25 minutes | **Cook time:** 30 minutes | **Serves:** 6

3 tablespoons salted butter
455 g sirloin steak, thinly sliced and cut into 2.5 cm pieces
1 medium onion, peeled and chopped
400 g sliced button mushrooms
2 cloves garlic, peeled and minced
1 tablespoon tomato paste
½ teaspoon salt
½ teaspoon ground black pepper
720 ml beef stock
2 teaspoons Worcestershire sauce
70 g dried egg noodles
120 g sour cream
2 tablespoons flour
10 g chopped fresh flat-leaf parsley

1. Move slider to AIR FRY/STOVETOP. Select SEAR/SAUTÉ and set to 3. Select START/STOP to begin preheating. Add the butter until melted, then add beef to the pot. Cook and stir often, until browned, about 10 minutes. Transfer to a plate and set aside. 2. Add onion and mushrooms to the pot. Cook until onions and mushrooms are tender, about 8 minutes. 3. Add garlic, tomato paste, salt, and pepper and cook for 1 minute, or until tomato paste is slightly darker in colour and fragrant. 4. Add stock and Worcestershire sauce to pot and stir well, making sure to scrape the bottom of pot to release any browned bits, then stir in noodles. Press START/STOP to turn off the SEAR/SAUTÉ function. 5. Close the lid and move slider to PRESSURE. Ensuring the pressure release valve is in the SEAL position. The temperature will default to HIGH, which is the correct setting. Set time to 6 minutes. Select START/STOP to begin cooking. 6. When cooking is complete, naturally release the pressure for 10 minutes. Then release the pressure quickly by turning the pressure release valve to the VENT position. Move slider to AIR FRY/ STOVETOP to unlock the lid, then carefully open it, and stir well. 7. In a small bowl combine sour cream and flour until smooth, then add 240 ml of cooking liquid and mix well. 8. Select SEAR/SAUTÉ and set to 3, whisk in sour cream mixture. Cook, stirring constantly, until soup is thick and bubbling, about 3 minutes. 9. Stir in browned beef and reserved juices and cook until beef is heated through, about 2 minutes. 10. Serve hot with parsley for garnish.
Per Serving: Calories 222; Fat 8.58g; Sodium 567mg; Carbs 15.18g; Fibre 1.1g; Sugar 2.42g; Protein 20.64g

Black-Eyed Peas and Ham Soup

Prep time: 10 minutes | **Cook time:** 16 minutes | **Serves:** 6

2 tablespoons olive oil
2 stalks celery, chopped
1 medium carrot, peeled and chopped
1 medium yellow onion, peeled and chopped
2 cloves garlic, peeled and lightly crushed
½ teaspoon salt
300 g diced smoked ham
455 g dried black-eyed peas, soaked overnight in water to cover and drained
½ teaspoon dried thyme leaves
960 ml ham stock or chicken stock

1. Add oil to the pot. Move slider to AIR FRY/STOVETOP. Select SEAR/SAUTÉ and set to 3. Select START/STOP to begin preheating. 2. Once the oil is hot, add celery, carrot, and onion to pot. Cook until vegetables are very tender, about 5 minutes. 3. Add garlic and salt and cook until fragrant, about 30 seconds. Press the START/STOP button. 4. Add ham, thyme, black-eyed peas, and stock to pot. Close the lid and move slider to PRESSURE. Ensuring the pressure release valve is in the SEAL position. The temperature will default to HIGH, which is the correct setting. Set time to 10 minutes. Select START/STOP to begin cooking. 5. When the time is up, let pressure release naturally, about 15–20 minutes, then open lid and stir well. Serve hot.
Per Serving: Calories 112; Fat 6g; Sodium 922mg; Carbs 10.07g; Fibre 2.7g; Sugar 5.08g; Protein 5.13g

Chapter 2 Soup, Chili and Stew Recipes

Cheesy Broccoli, Carrot and Cauliflower Soup

Prep time: 15 minutes | **Cook time:** 15 minutes | **Serves:** 2

½ tablespoon oil	90 g chopped cauliflower (including stems)
½ large onion, chopped	200 g shredded low-fat Cheddar cheese
120 g chopped carrots	½ teaspoon paprika
2 garlic cloves, minced	¼ teaspoon nutmeg
2 tablespoons flour	120 ml whole milk
480 ml Vegetable Stock	Salt
180 g chopped broccoli (including stems), plus 90 g florets reserved	Freshly ground black pepper

1. Move slider to AIR FRY/STOVETOP. Select SEAR/SAUTÉ and set to 3. Select START/STOP to begin preheating. Heat the oil and add the onion and carrots and cook until softened, 3 to 4 minutes. 2. Add the garlic and flour and stir for 1 minute. Add the stock and continue stirring until no flour lumps remain. Press START/STOP to turn off the SEAR/SAUTÉ function. 3. Add the chopped broccoli and the chopped cauliflower to the pot. 4. Close the lid and move slider to PRESSURE. Ensuring the pressure release valve is in the SEAL position. The temperature will default to HIGH, which is the correct setting. Set time to 8 minutes. Select START/STOP to begin cooking. 5. When cooking is complete, release the pressure quickly by turning the pressure release valve to the VENT position. Move slider to the right to unlock the lid, then carefully open it. 6. Using a blender, carefully purée the soup until smooth. 7. Move slider to AIR FRY/STOVETOP. Select SEAR/SAUTÉ and set to 3. Add the Cheddar cheese, paprika, and nutmeg. Press START/STOP to begin cooking and stir until fully combined and the cheese is melted. 8. Stir in the milk and season with salt and pepper. Press START/STOP to end the cooking function add the reserved 90 g of broccoli florets and stir well, then loosely cover the pot and let sit for 4 to 5 minutes before serving.

Per Serving: Calories 679; Fat 35.74g; Sodium 1967mg; Carbs 44.5g; Fibre 7.8g; Sugar 19.51g; Protein 46.2g

Herbed Kidney Bean and Sausage Soup

Prep time: 15 minutes | **Cook time:** 45 minutes | **Serves:** 6

225 g Italian sausage	455 g dried kidney beans, soaked overnight in water to cover and drained
1 large yellow onion, peeled and chopped	4 sprigs fresh thyme
180 g roughly chopped cabbage	10 g roughly chopped fresh flat-leaf parsley
2 cloves garlic, peeled and minced	1.9 L water
1 teaspoon ground fennel	½ teaspoon salt
½ teaspoon dried oregano	
1 teaspoon smoked paprika	

1. Add sausage to the pot of your Ninja XL Pressure Cooker. Move slider to AIR FRY/STOVETOP. Select SEAR/SAUTÉ and set to Lo1. Select START/STOP to begin cooking, crumbling into 1 cm pieces, until sausage is browned, about 8 minutes. 2. Add onion and cook, stirring often, until tender, about 5 minutes. Add cabbage, garlic, oregano, fennel, and paprika and cook 2 minutes until garlic and spices are fragrant. 3. Add beans, thyme, and chopped parsley to pot and toss to coat in onion and spices. Add water, then press the START/STOP button. 4. Close the lid and move slider to PRESSURE. Ensuring the pressure release valve is in the SEAL position. 5. The temperature will default to HIGH, which is the correct setting. Set time to 30 minutes. Select START/STOP to begin cooking. 6. When the time is up, let pressure release naturally, about 15 minutes. Uncover, remove thyme sprigs, stir in salt, and serve hot.

Per Serving: Calories 167; Fat 11.05g; Sodium 553mg; Carbs 10.34g; Fibre 2.6g; Sugar 1.87g; Protein 9.37g

Chapter 3 Vegetable and Sides Recipes

Simple Corn on the Cob (Four Ways)

Prep time: 5 minutes | **Cook time:** 2 minutes | **Serves:** 4

For the Corn:
4 ears corn, shucked
For Mexican Corn on the Cob:
80 g mayonnaise
10 g finely chopped fresh coriander
2 teaspoons ground New Mexican chili powder
50 g crumbled aged Cotija or feta cheese
For Maple-Barbecue Corn on the Cob:
4 tablespoons room-temperature butter
2 tablespoons maple syrup
4 teaspoons thick barbecue sauce
Garlic salt
For Hot Wings–Style Corn on the Cob:
4 tablespoons butter, at room temperature
2 tablespoons hot sauce
4 teaspoons honey
55 g crumbled blue cheese
1¼ teaspoons celery salt
For French Corn on the Cob:
120 g soft herb and garlic cheese spread (such as Boursin), at room temperature
2 tablespoons finely chopped fresh chives
Freshly ground black pepper

1. Place the bottom layer of the Deluxe Reversible Rack in the lower position in the pot. and pour in 360 ml warm water. Place the on the rack (cutting the corn cobs in half if necessary to make them fit). 2. Close the lid and move slider to PRESSURE. Ensuring the pressure release valve is in the SEAL position. The temperature will default to HIGH, which is the correct setting. Set time to 2 minutes. Select START/STOP to begin cooking. 3. When the cooking time is up, quick-release the pressure. 4. For Mexican corn, spread the mayonnaise on the corn with a rubber spatula and sprinkle with the coriander , chili powder, and cheese. 5. For maple-barbecue corn, combine the butter, maple syrup, and barbecue sauce in a medium bowl. Spread the mixture on the corn and sprinkle with garlic salt. 6. For hot wings–style corn, in a medium bowl, combine the butter, hot sauce, and honey and mix well. Spread on the corn and then roll the cobs in the blue cheese and sprinkle with the celery salt. 7. For French corn, spread the cheese spread all over the cobs. Roll in the chives and season with pepper.

Per Serving: Calories 198; Fat 11.03g; Sodium 431mg; Carbs 20.17g; Fibre 3.1g; Sugar 3.18g; Protein 7.83g

White Rice with Peas and Swiss Chard

Prep time: 15 minutes | **Cook time:** 15 minutes | **Serves:** 4

185 g dried black-eyed peas, soaked overnight or quick-soaked
2½ tablespoons olive oil
1 medium yellow onion, chopped
1 red pepper, chopped
3 teaspoons salt-free Cajun seasoning
Optional Garnish:
Hot sauce

300 g long-grain white rice, rinsed and drained
Salt
1 bunch Swiss chard, centre rib and stem discarded, leaves torn into bite-size pieces
Freshly ground black pepper

1. Drain the beans and set aside. Put 1½ tablespoons of the oil in the pot, Move slider to AIR FRY/STOVETOP. Select SEAR/SAUTÉ and set to Hi 5. Select START/STOP to begin cooking. 2. Add the onion, pepper, and Cajun seasoning and cook, stirring often, until the onion is tender, 4 minutes. Press START/STOP. Add the beans and 300 ml water and stir to combine. 3. Then place the bottom layer of the Deluxe Reversible Rack in the lower position in the pot. 4. Combine the rice with 360 ml cold water, the remaining tablespoon of oil, and a good pinch of salt in the multi-purpose pan. Place the pan, uncovered, on the rack over the bean mixture. 5. Close the lid and move slider to PRESSURE. Ensuring the pressure release valve is in the SEAL position. The temperature will default to HIGH, which is the correct setting. Set time to 4 minutes. Select START/STOP to begin cooking. 6. When the cooking time is up, let the pressure come down naturally for 10 minutes, and then quick-release any remaining pressure. 7. Remove the rice in the pan, fluff with a fork, cover loosely, and set aside. Add the Swiss chard to the pot and stir gently to combine it with the black-eyed peas. 8. Move slider to AIR FRY/STOVETOP. Select SEAR/SAUTÉ and set to 3. Simmer until the chard is wilted, 5 minutes. Season with salt and pepper. 9. Serve the rice topped with the black-eyed pea mixture and optional hot sauce on the side.

Per Serving: Calories 348; Fat 9.03g; Sodium 937mg; Carbs 59.95g; Fibre 1.9g; Sugar 2.08g; Protein 5.84g

Spanish Rice with Pepper s

Prep time: 5 minutes | **Cook time:** 10 minutes | **Serves:** 4

2 tablespoons olive oil
1 small onion, finely chopped
150 g chopped green pepper

300 g long-grain rice, rinsed and drained
2 tablespoons taco seasoning
160 ml V8 tomato juice

1. Move slider to AIR FRY/STOVETOP. Select SEAR/SAUTÉ and set to 3. Select START/STOP to begin preheating. Heat the oil and add the onion and pepper and cook, stirring frequently, until tender, 4 minutes. Press START/STOP. Add the rice and taco seasoning and stir to coat the rice with the vegetables and oil. 2. Add 420 ml water and the tomato juice and stir to combine. Close the lid and move slider to PRESSURE, Ensuring the pressure release valve is in the SEAL position. The temperature will default to HIGH, which is the correct setting. Set time to 4 minutes. Select START/STOP to begin cooking. 3. When cooking is complete, let the pressure come down naturally for 5 minutes and then quick-release the remaining pressure. 4. Fluff with a fork and serve.

Per Serving: Calories 348; Fat 8.92g; Sodium 361mg; Carbs 60.16g; Fibre 4.2g; Sugar 3.39g; Protein 6.44g

Cheesy Tortellini Alfredo and Peas

Prep time: 15 minutes | **Cook time:** 12 minutes | **Serves:** 4

455 g dried cheese tortellini (such as Barilla Three Cheese Tortellini)
720 ml store-bought vegetable or chicken stock, or homemade
2 medium garlic cloves, chopped
2 teaspoons olive oil
Salt and freshly ground black pepper
80 g frozen peas, thawed
360 g whipping cream
2 teaspoons finely grated lemon zest
50 g grated Parmesan cheese

1. Add the tortellini, olive oil, stock, garlic, 1 teaspoon salt, and a pinch of pepper to the pot. 2. Close the lid and move slider to PRESSURE. Ensuring the pressure release valve is in the SEAL position. The temperature will default to HIGH, which is the correct setting. Set time to 10 minutes. Select START/STOP to begin cooking. 3. When cooking is complete, naturally release the pressure for 10 minutes. Then release the pressure quickly by moving the pressure release valve to the VENT position. Move slider to AIR FRY/ STOVETOP to unlock the lid, then carefully open it. 4. Add the peas, cream, and lemon zest. Move slider to AIR FRY/ STOVETOP. Select SEAR/SAUTÉ and set to 3. Select START/STOP to begin cooking. Stirring occasionally, until the sauce thickens slightly, 2 minutes. Press START/STOP. Add the cheese and stir gently to combine. 5. Serve immediately.

Per Serving: Calories 677; Fat 51.73g; Sodium 826`mg; Carbs 26.82g; Fibre 2.1g; Sugar 13.89g; Protein 28.19g

Cheese Pasta with Broccoli

Prep time: 15 minutes | **Cook time:** 5 minutes | **Serves:** 4

300 g dry elbow macaroni or rotini pasta
4 teaspoons olive oil
1¼ teaspoons dry mustard
Salt and freshly ground black pepper
1 large (200 g) broccoli crown, left whole
100 g chive and onion cream cheese spread
150 g grated sharp cheddar cheese

1. Add the pasta, 720 ml water, mustard, the oil, and 1 teaspoon salt to the pot and stir well. Place the broccoli on top of the pasta, pushing the stalk into the pasta and liquid but leaving the florets above the mixture. 2. Close the lid and move slider to PRESSURE. Ensuring the pressure release valve is in the SEAL position. adjust to LOW pressure and set time to 5 minutes. Select START/STOP to begin cooking. 3. When cooking is complete, release the pressure quickly by turning the pressure release valve to the VENT position. Move slider to the right to unlock the lid, then carefully open it. Transfer the broccoli to a cutting board. Chop the firm stem into bite-size pieces and leave the florets whole; set aside. 4. Add the cream cheese to the pasta and stir with a rubber spatula until melted. Add the cheddar in two additions, stirring after each addition. 5. Remove the pot from the appliance, add the broccoli to the pot, and stir to combine; the broccoli will fall apart into tiny pieces. 6. Season with salt and pepper and serve right away.

Per Serving: Calories 658; Fat 31.44g; Sodium 840mg; Carbs 66.92g; Fibre 4.3g; Sugar 3.69g; Protein 26.98g

Lemony Mushroom and Leeks Risotto

Prep time: 15 minutes | **Cook time:** 18 minutes | **Serves:** 4

2 tablespoons olive oil
2 medium leeks, white and light green parts only, halved lengthwise, rinsed, and chopped
400 g mixed wild mushrooms, sliced
1 tablespoon chopped fresh thyme
Salt
200 g Arborio rice
720 ml store-bought mushroom stock or vegetable stock, or homemade
50 g grated Parmesan cheese
Finely grated zest and juice of ½ lemon
Freshly ground black pepper

1. Move slider to AIR FRY/STOVETOP. Select SEAR/SAUTÉ and set to 3. Select START/STOP to begin preheating. Heat the oil and add the leeks and cook, stirring occasionally, until tender, 3 minutes. 2. Add the mushrooms, thyme, and a generous pinch of salt and cook, stirring occasionally, until the mushrooms give off their liquid and begin to brown, 7 minutes. Press START/STOP. Set aside ¼ of the mushroom mixture for garnish. 3. Add the rice and stir to coat the grains with the vegetables and oil. Add the stock and stir to combine. 4. Close the lid and move slider to PRESSURE. Ensuring the pressure release valve is in the SEAL position. The temperature will default to HIGH, which is the correct setting. Set time to 8 minutes. Select START/STOP to begin cooking. 5. When cooking is complete, release the pressure quickly by turning the pressure release valve to the VENT position. Move slider to the right to unlock the lid, then carefully open it. 6. Add the cheese, lemon zest, and lemon juice and stir to combine. Season with salt and pepper. 7. Serve, garnished with the reserved sautéed mushrooms and leeks.

Per Serving: Calories 329; Fat 16.97g; Sodium 591mg; Carbs 46.23g; Fibre 8.9g; Sugar 21g; Protein 11.22g

Indian–Spiced Basmati Rice with Peas

Prep time: 10 minutes | **Cook time:** 7 minutes | **Serves:** 4

2 tablespoons rapeseed oil
3 medium garlic cloves, finely chopped
1 tablespoon finely chopped fresh ginger
300 g basmati rice, rinsed and drained
1½ teaspoons garam masala or curry powder
½ teaspoon ground turmeric
Salt
130 g frozen peas

1. Move slider to AIR FRY/STOVETOP. Select SEAR/SAUTÉ and set to 3. Select START/STOP to begin preheating. Heat the oil and add the garlic and ginger and cook, stirring often, until fragrant, 45 seconds. Press START/STOP. 2. Add the rice, garam marsala, and turmeric and toss to coat. Add 360 ml water and ¾ teaspoon salt. Sprinkle the peas over the top of the rice. 3. Close the lid and move slide to PRESSURE. Ensuring the pressure release valve is in the SEAL position. 4. The temperature will default to HIGH, which is the correct setting. Set time to 6 minutes. Select START/STOP to begin cooking. 5. When cooking is complete, naturally release the pressure for 10 minutes. Then release the pressure quickly by turning the pressure release valve to the VENT position. Move slider to AIR FRY/ STOVETOP to unlock the lid, then carefully open it. 6. Fluff with a fork and serve.

Per Serving: Calories 124; Fat 7.34g; Sodium 352mg; Carbs 14.52g; Fibre 2.2g; Sugar 8.85g; Protein 1.73g

Mustard Potato and Bacon Salad

Prep time: 10 minutes | **Cook time:** 15 minutes | **Serves:** 6

200 g applewood-smoked bacon, chopped	2 teaspoons caraway seeds
120 ml store-bought chicken stock , or homemade	½ teaspoon salt, plus more for seasoning
6 tablespoons white wine vinegar	1.2 kg small red potatoes, unpeeled, cut into 2 cm chunks
2½ tablespoons grainy mustard	75 g finely chopped sweet onion
2 tablespoons packed light brown sugar	Freshly ground black pepper

1. Add the bacon to the pot, Move slider to AIR FRY/STOVETOP. Select SEAR/SAUTÉ and set to 3. Select START/STOP to begin cooking. Stirring frequently, until crisp and browned, 8 minutes. Press START/STOP. 2. With a slotted spoon, transfer the bacon to a paper towel–lined plate. Reserve 2 tablespoons of the drippings in a small bowl for the dressing and discard the remaining drippings. 3. Put the stock , vinegar, caraway seeds, mustard, brown sugar, and ½ teaspoon salt in the pot and whisk to combine. 4. Place the Cook & Crisp Basket in the pot and add the potatoes to the basket. Close the lid and move slider to PRESSURE. 5. Ensuring the pressure release valve is in the SEAL position. The temperature will default to HIGH, which is the correct setting. Set time to 7 minutes. Select START/STOP to begin cooking. 6. When the cooking time is up, quick-release the pressure. Carefully remove the basket and turn the potatoes into a large bowl. 7. Pour the cooking liquid and the reserved bacon drippings over the potatoes. 8. Add the onion, season with salt and several grinds of pepper, and toss gently with a rubber spatula to combine. Serve warm.
Per Serving: Calories 574; Fat 11.87g; Sodium 959mg; Carbs 113.73g; Fibre 5.6g; Sugar 76.18g; Protein 9.06g

Lima Beans with Bacon & Tomato

Prep time: 10 minutes | **Cook time:** 20 minutes | **Serves:** 12

8 bacon strips, cut into 2.5 cm pieces	2 tsp. sugar
140 g finely chopped onion	2 tsp. salt
80 g finely chopped celery	¼ tsp. pepper
75 g finely chopped green pepper	2 cans diced tomatoes, undrained
2 garlic cloves, minced	1 kg frozen lima beans, thawed
2 tsp. flour	

1. Move slider to AIR FRY/STOVETOP. Select SEAR/SAUTÉ and set to 3. Select START/STOP to begin preheating. 2. Then add the bacon, onion, celery and green pepper and cook until bacon is crisp and vegetables are tender. 3. Add garlic; cook 1 minute longer. Stir in flour, sugar, salt and pepper. Add tomatoes and bring to a boil, stirring constantly; cook and stir 1-2 minutes or until thickened. Stir in beans. Press START/STOP. 4. Close the lid and move slider to PRESSURE. Ensuring the pressure release valve is in the SEAL position. The temperature will default to HIGH, which is the correct setting. Set time to 10 minutes. Select START/STOP to begin cooking. 5. When cooking is complete, release the pressure quickly by turning the pressure release valve to the VENT position. Move slider to the right to unlock the lid, then carefully open it. Serve warm.
Per Serving: Calories 182; Fat 1.73g; Sodium 615mg; Carbs 33.99g; Fibre 8.6g; Sugar 2.79g; Protein 9.69g

Cheesy Spaghetti with Sausage and Broccolini

Prep time: 15 minutes | **Cook time:** 15 minutes | **Serves:** 4-6

455 g hot or sweet Italian sausage, casing removed	½ teaspoon red pepper flakes
2 tablespoons extra-virgin olive oil, divided, plus more to serve	Salt and ground black pepper
	455 g spaghetti, broken in half
6 medium garlic cloves, finely chopped	200 g broccolini, trimmed and finely chopped
2 tablespoons fennel seeds	25 g Parmesan cheese, finely grated, plus more to serve

1. In a medium bowl, combine the sausage with 80 ml water. Stir with a fork until well combined. Move slider to AIR FRY/STOVETOP. Select SEAR/SAUTÉ and set to Lo1. Select START/STOP to begin preheating. 2. Add 1 tablespoon of oil and the sausage to the preheated pot and cook, stirring and breaking the meat into small pieces, until the sausage is no longer pink, about 5 minutes. 3. Stir in the garlic, fennel seeds and pepper flakes, then cook until fragrant, about 30 seconds. Add 1.2 L water and 1 teaspoon salt; stir to combine, then distribute in an even layer. 4. Add the pasta, placing the strands horizontally so they lay flat, then press them into the liquid until submerged. Press START/STOP. 5. Close the lid and move slider to PRESSURE; Ensuring the pressure release valve is in the SEAL position. The temperature will default to HIGH, which is the correct setting. Set time to 3 minutes. Select START/STOP to begin cooking. 6. When cooking is complete, release the pressure quickly by turning the pressure release valve to the VENT position. Move slider to the right to unlock the lid, then carefully open it. 7. Using tongs, toss and stir the mixture to separate the strands of pasta, then stir in the broccolini. 8. Re-cover without locking the lid in place and let stand until the broccolini is tender and the pasta is al dente, about 5 minutes. 9. Stir in the parmesan and the remaining 1 tablespoon oil. Season with salt and pepper, then transfer to a serving dish. Drizzle with oil and serve with additional parmesan on the side.

Per Serving: Calories 387; Fat 15.13g; Sodium 702mg; Carbs 30.94g; Fibre 5.4g; Sugar 1.74g; Protein 33.68g

Kale and Edamame Salad with Sesame Ginger Dressing

Prep time: 10 minutes | **Cook time:** 0 minutes | **Serves:** 6

180 g baby kale salad blend	90 g fresh bean sprouts
1 can garbanzo beans or chickpeas, rinsed and drained	60 g salted peanuts
250 g frozen shelled edamame thawed	2 green onions, diagonally sliced
3 clementines, peeled and segmented	120 g sesame ginger salad dressing

1. Divide salad blend among six bowls. Top with all remaining ingredients except salad dressing. 2. Serve with dressing.

Per Serving: Calories 374; Fat 24.2g; Sodium 424mg; Carbs 28.36g; Fibre 9g; Sugar 10.24g; Protein 16.73g

Spiced Corn with Jalapeno-Peppers

Prep time: 15 minutes | **Cook time:** 20 minutes | **Serves:** 4

4 ears fresh sweet corn
2 jalapeno peppers
3 tbsp. rapeseed oil, divided
¾ tsp. salt, divided
30 g panko (Japanese) bread crumbs
½ tsp. smoked paprika
½ tsp. dried Mexican oregano
100 g cream cheese, softened
60 g media crema table cream or sour cream thinned with
1 tsp. low fat milk
2 tbsp. lime juice
Ground chipotle pepper or chili powder
Chopped fresh coriander, optional

1. Husk corn. Rub corn and jalapenos with 2 tbsp. rapeseed oil. Place the Cook & Crisp Basket in the pot. Place the corn and jalapenos in the basket. 2. Close the lid and move slider to AIR FRY/STOVETOP. Select AIR FRY. Set the temp to 360°F and set time to 10-12 minutes. Press START/STOP to begin cooking. 3. When cooking time is up, take out the jalapenos and remove its skin, seeds and membranes when it's cool enough to handle; chop finely. Set aside. 4. Place the corn in a dish and sprinkle with ½ tsp. salt. Add oil to the pot, move slider to AIR FRY/STOVETOP. Select SEAR/SAUTÉ and set to 3. Select START/STOP to begin preheating. 5. Once the oil is hot, add panko; cook and stir until starting to brown. Add paprika and oregano; cook until crumbs are toasted and fragrant. 6. Meanwhile, combine cream cheese, crema, lime juice and remaining salt; spread over corn. Sprinkle with bread crumbs, jalapenos, chipotle powder and, spread the coriander on top if desired.

Per Serving: Calories 340; Fat 23.34g; Sodium 601mg; Carbs 31.2g; Fibre 4.3g; Sugar 6.72g; Protein 7.37g

Jalapeno & Cotija Cheese Potato Pie

Prep time: 20 minutes | **Cook time:** 50 minutes | **Serves:** 8

1.3 kg red potatoes, peeled and thinly sliced
55 g butter, melted
½ tsp. salt
¼ tsp. pepper
2 jalapeno peppers, seeded and minced
125 g crumbled cotija cheese or crumbled feta cheese
Salsa and sour cream, optional

1. Place the multi-purpose pan on the bottom layer of the Deluxe Reversible Rack in the lower position in the pot. Line the pan with parchment paper. 2. Place the potatoes, butter, salt and pepper in a large bowl; toss to coat. Layer ⅓ of the potatoes evenly in the pan. Sprinkle with ⅓ of the jalapenos and ⅓ of the cheese. Repeat layers. Top with remaining potatoes and jalapenos. 3. Close the lid and move slider to the AIR FRY/ STOVETOP. Preheat the pot by selecting BAKE/ ROAST. Setting temperature to 190°C, and setting time to 35 minutes. Select START/STOP to begin cooking. 4. When the cooking time is up, top with remaining cheese. cook for 15-20 minutes longer or until potatoes are tender. Let stand 5 minutes. Serve with salsa and sour cream, if desired.

Per Serving: Calories 209; Fat 10.51g; Sodium 360mg; Carbs 23.47g; Fibre 2.5g; Sugar 2.49g; Protein 6.25g

Cheese Broccoli Potato Cake

Prep time: 10 minutes | **Cook time:** 16 minutes | **Serves:** 4

240 ml water
420 g mashed potatoes
1 medium head broccoli, chopped
½ teaspoon salt
¼ teaspoon black pepper
¼ teaspoon garlic powder
100 g shredded Cheddar cheese

1. Pour water to the pot and place the bottom layer of the Deluxe Reversible Rack in the lower position in the pot. 2. Spoon mashed potatoes into a cake pan that can fit the pot. 3. In a medium bowl, combine broccoli with salt, pepper, and garlic powder, toss well. Place the seasoned broccoli on top of mashed potatoes. 4. Sprinkle cheese over broccoli. Cover cake pan tightly with foil. Create a foil sling and carefully place the cake pan on the rack. 5. Close the lid and move slider to PRESSURE. Ensuring the pressure release valve is in the SEAL position. The temperature will default to HIGH, which is the correct setting. Set time to 16 minutes. Select START/STOP to begin cooking. 6. When cooking is complete, release the pressure quickly by turning the pressure release valve to the VENT position. Move slider to the right to unlock the lid, then carefully open it. 7. Remove cake pan using foil sling and then remove foil from top of pan and serve.
Per Serving: Calories 195; Fat 11.28g; Sodium 512mg; Carbs 14.08g; Fibre 2g; Sugar 0.72g; Protein 9.82g

Black Bean and Rice–Stuffed Peppers

Prep time: 10 minutes | **Cook time:** 8 minutes | **Serves:** 4

240 ml water
½ can black beans, rinsed and drained
1 (100 g) can mild diced green chilies
250 g cooked rice
120 g frozen corn kernels, thawed
4 large green peppers
50 g shredded Cheddar cheese

1. Pour water into the pot of your Ninja XL Pressure Cooker and place the bottom layer of the Deluxe Reversible Rack in the lower position in the pot. 2. In a medium bowl, mix together beans, green chilies, rice, and corn. Set aside. 3. Slice tops of pepper s off and remove seeds from inside peppers. 4. Scoop black bean mixture into each pepper and fill just to the top. Carefully place stuffed peppers on the rack. 5. Close the lid and move slider to PRESSURE. Ensuring the pressure release valve is in the SEAL position. The temperature will default to HIGH, which is the correct setting. Set time to 8 minutes. Select START/STOP to begin cooking. 6. When cooking is complete, release the pressure quickly by turning the pressure release valve to the VENT position. Move slider to the right to unlock the lid, then carefully open it. 7. Remove peppers and sprinkle with cheese. Serve hot.
Per Serving: Calories 597; Fat 13.9g; Sodium 188mg; Carbs 96.45g; Fibre 24.8g; Sugar 6.08g; Protein 33.55g

Cheesy Alfredo Pasta with Carrots & Broccoli

Prep time: 10 minutes | **Cook time:** 12 minutes | **Serves:** 4

2 tablespoons olive oil
1 medium head broccoli, chopped
3 medium carrots, sliced
2 cloves garlic, minced
½ teaspoon salt
½ teaspoon black pepper
¼ teaspoon onion powder

960 ml vegetable stock
455 g fettuccine
2 tablespoons butter, cubed
240 ml whole milk
75 g grated Parmesan cheese
120 ml cold water
1 tablespoon cornflour

1. Move slider to AIR FRY/STOVETOP. Select SEAR/SAUTÉ and set to 3. Select START/STOP to begin cooking. Heat the oil in the pot, add the broccoli and carrots. Stirring occasionally, 5 minutes. 2. Add garlic, salt, pepper, and onion powder. Cook an additional 30 seconds. Press START/STOP. 3. Pour in stock and deglaze bottom of pot. Break fettuccine in half and place in pot. Top fettuccine with cubed butter. 4. Close the lid and move slider to PRESSURE. Ensuring the pressure release valve is in the SEAL position. The temperature will default to HIGH, which is the correct setting. Set time to 6 minutes. Select START/STOP to begin cooking. 5. When cooking is complete, release the pressure quickly by turning the pressure release valve to the VENT position. Move slider to the right to unlock the lid, then carefully open it. 6. Pour in milk and Parmesan and mix until fully combined. 7. In a small bowl, whisk together water and cornflour . Mix into Alfredo pasta and stir for 1 minute. Serve hot.
Per Serving: Calories 504; Fat 29.53g; Sodium 979mg; Carbs 43.32g; Fibre 4.6g; Sugar 17.09g; Protein 18.97g

Black Bean & Brown Rice Casserole

Prep time: 10 minutes | **Cook time:** 8 minutes | **Serves:** 4

240ml water
500 g cooked brown rice
1 can black beans
1 can sweet corn kernels
1 (100 g) can mild diced green chilies

½ teaspoon salt
½ teaspoon dried oregano
½ teaspoon cumin
½ teaspoon red pepper flakes

1. Pour water into the pot and place the bottom layer of the Deluxe Reversible Rack in the lower position in the pot. 2. In a metal bowl, combine rice, black beans, salt, corn, cumin, chilies, oregano, and red pepper flakes and mix. Cover bowl tightly with foil. 3. Create a foil sling and carefully lower bowl on the rack. 4. Close the lid and move slider to PRESSURE. Ensuring the pressure release valve is in the SEAL position. The temperature will default to HIGH, which is the correct setting. Set time to 8 minutes. Select START/STOP to begin cooking. 5. When cooking is complete, release the pressure quickly by turning the pressure release valve to the VENT position. Move slider to the right to unlock the lid, then carefully open it. 6. Remove bowl using foil sling and then remove foil from bowl and serve.
Per Serving: Calories 422; Fat 4.06g; Sodium 509mg; Carbs 88.63g; Fibre 6.8g; Sugar 3.53g; Protein 10.02g

Vegetarian Gumbo with Rice

Prep time: 20 minutes | **Cook time:** 30 minutes | **Serves:** 8

- 60 ml vegetable oil
- 30 g flour
- 4 stalks celery, chopped
- 1 large yellow onion, peeled and diced
- 1 large green pepper, seeded and diced
- 180 g sliced fresh okra
- 200 g button mushrooms, quartered
- 3 cloves garlic, peeled and minced
- ½ teaspoon dried thyme
- ¼ teaspoon Creole seasoning
- 2 bay leaves
- 2 teaspoons Creole mustard
- 960 ml vegetable stock
- 1 medium courgette, diced
- 1 can red beans, drained and rinsed
- ¼ teaspoon salt
- ¼ teaspoon ground black pepper
- 500 g cooked long-grain rice

1. Move slider to AIR FRY/STOVETOP. Select SEAR/SAUTÉ and set to 3. Select START/STOP to begin preheating. 2. Heat the oil and add flour and cook, stirring constantly, until flour is medium brown in colour, about 15 minutes. 3. Add celery, onion, green pepper, okra, mushrooms, and garlic. Cook, stirring constantly, until the vegetables are tender, about 8 minutes. 4. Add thyme, Creole seasoning, bay leaves, Creole mustard, and stock and stir well, making sure nothing is stuck to the bottom of the pot. Add courgette and beans and stir well. Press START/STOP. 5. Close the lid and move slider to PRESSURE. Ensuring the pressure release valve is in the SEAL position. The temperature will default to HIGH, which is the correct setting. Set time to 5 minutes. Select START/STOP to begin cooking. 6. When cooking is complete, release the pressure quickly by turning the pressure release valve to the VENT position. Move slider to the right to unlock the lid, then carefully open it. 7. Discard bay leaves, and stir in salt and black pepper. Serve hot over rice.

Per Serving: Calories 324; Fat 9.93g; Sodium 469mg; Carbs 54.26g; Fibre 8.9g; Sugar 5.02g; Protein 10.11g

Rosemary Navy Beans

Prep time: 10 minutes | **Cook time:** 30 minutes | **Serves:** 8

- 455 g dry navy beans
- 1.4 L vegetable stock
- 6 springs fresh rosemary
- 1 tablespoon onion powder
- 2 teaspoons garlic powder
- ½ teaspoon salt
- 1 bay leaf

1. Combine all ingredients in the pot. Close the lid and move slider to PRESSURE. Ensuring the pressure release valve is in the SEAL position. The temperature will default to HIGH, which is the correct setting. Set time to 30 minutes. Select START/STOP to begin cooking. 2. When cooking is complete, release the pressure quickly by turning the pressure release valve to the VENT position. Move slider to the right to unlock the lid, then carefully open it. 3. Serve warm.

Per Serving: Calories 266; Fat 2.49g; Sodium 574mg; Carbs 47.08g; Fibre 11.2g; Sugar 4.89g; Protein 16.13g

Autumn Potatoes Egg Salad

Prep time: 10 minutes | **Cook time:** 5 minutes | **Serves:** 4-6

360 ml water
4 eggs
6 medium potatoes, peeled and cut into 4 cm cubes
1 tbsp dill pickle juice
240 g homemade mayonnaise

2 tbsp parsley, finely chopped
35 g onion, finely chopped
1 tbsp mustard
Salt and ground black pepper to taste

1. Pour the water into the pot. Then place the bottom layer of the Deluxe Reversible Rack in the lower position in the pot. 2. Place the eggs and potatoes on the rack. Close the lid and move slider to PRESSURE. Ensuring the pressure release valve is in the SEAL position. The temperature will default to HIGH, which is the correct setting. Set time to 5 minutes. Select START/STOP to begin cooking. 3. When cooking is complete, release the pressure quickly by turning the pressure release valve to the VENT position. Move slider to the right to unlock the lid, then carefully open it. 4. Transfer the eggs to the bowl of cold water. Wait 2-3 minutes. 5. In another bowl, combine the dill pickle juice, mayo, parsley, onion, and mustard. Mix well. 6. Add the potatoes and gently stir to coat with the sauce. Peel eggs, chop and add to the salad. Stir well. 7. Season with salt and pepper, stir and serve.

Per Serving: Calories 611; Fat 23.59g; Sodium 735mg; Carbs 81.96g; Fibre 10.9g; Sugar 5.42g; Protein 19.51g

Chapter 4 Poultry Mains Recipes

Greek Chicken and Mixed Greens Salad

Prep time: 10 minutes | **Cook time:** 17 minutes | **Serves:** 4

1 tbsp sour cream
60 ml extra-virgin olive oil, plus more for sautéing
1 clove garlic, grated
½ tsp fresh thyme leaves
¼ tsp crushed red pepper flakes
Salad:
2 jarred roasted red peppers, thinly sliced
½ red onion, thinly sliced
2 Persian cucumbers, thinly sliced
2 tbsp pitted and sliced black olives
2 tbsp pitted and sliced green olives
425 g mixed greens
Salt
Freshly ground black pepper
½ tsp dried oregano
2 large boneless, skinless chicken breasts
Juice of ½ lemon

Crumbled feta cheese, for topping
Juice of ½ lemon
1 tbsp olive oil
Salt
Freshly ground black pepper

1. In a gallon-size resealable plastic bag, combine the sour cream, olive oil, thyme, red pepper flakes, garlic, salt and black pepper to taste and oregano. Seal the bag and shake until the entire marinade is combined. 2. Add the chicken breasts to the marinade. Store in the fridge for at least 15 minutes, or up to 3 hours at the most. 3. After the chicken has marinated, place about 1 teaspoon of olive oil in the pot. Move slider to AIR FRY/STOVETOP. Select SEAR/SAUTÉ and set to 3. Select START/STOP to begin cooking. 4. Use tongs to remove the chicken breasts from the marinade and add them to the pot. Sauté for about 3 minutes per side. 5. Use a silicone spatula to get under the chicken if it sticks a little. Remove the chicken from the pot and transfer to a plate. 6. Press START/STOP and add the lemon juice to the pot. Scrape up the browned bits of flavour from the bottom of the pot, using a wooden spoon or silicone spatula. 7. Return the chicken to the pot. Close the lid and move slider to PRESSURE. Ensuring the pressure release valve is in the SEAL position. The temperature will default to HIGH, which is the correct setting. Set time to 10 minutes. Select START/STOP to begin cooking. 8. When cooking is complete, release the pressure quickly by turning the pressure release valve to the VENT position. Move slider to the right to unlock the lid, then carefully open it. 9. Let the chicken rest for 4 to 5 minutes before removing and slicing. 10. Assemble the salad: In a large serving bowl, toss the roasted red peppers, cucumbers, red onion, olives and mixed greens. Slice the chicken breasts. 11. Top the salad with the chicken and then the feta cheese, lemon juice and olive oil. Season with a little bit of salt and black pepper.

Per Serving: Calories 555; Fat 39.65g; Sodium 1254mg; Carbs 11.95g; Fibre 5.1g; Sugar 4.77g; Protein 38.76g

Teriyaki Chicken Wings

Prep time: 10 minutes | **Cook time:** 10 minutes | **Serves:** 6

1.3 kg "party" chicken wings (separated at the joints)
120 ml plus 2 tablespoons low-sodium soy sauce
Salt and freshly ground black pepper
75 g packed brown sugar
2 tablespoons cider vinegar or rice vinegar
4 teaspoons finely chopped fresh ginger
4 medium garlic cloves, finely chopped
1 tablespoon cornflour

1. Pour 360 ml water into the pot and place a Cook & Crisp Basket inside. In a large bowl, toss the wings with 2 tablespoons of the soy sauce and season with salt and pepper. Place the wings on the basket. 2. Close the lid and move slider to PRESSURE. Ensuring the pressure release valve is in the SEAL position. The temperature will default to HIGH, which is the correct setting. Set time to 5 minutes. Select START/STOP to begin cooking. 3. Preheat the grill er and move an oven rack so that it is 10 cm below the grill er element. Cover a baking sheet with foil and grease with cooking spray. 4. When the cooking time is up, quick-release the pressure. Transfer the chicken wings to the prepared baking sheet. Discard the cooking liquid and remove the basket from the pot. 5. Add the remaining soy sauce, vinegar, the brown sugar, ginger, and garlic to the pot. 6. Move slider to AIR FRY/STOVETOP. Select SEAR/SAUTÉ and set to 3. Select START/STOP to begin cooking. Bring to a simmer, stirring often, until the sugar has dissolved, 3 minutes. 7. In a small bowl, mix the cornflour with 1 tablespoon water. 8. Add the cornflour mixture to the pot and cook, stirring constantly, until the sauce has thickened, 1 minute. 9. Spoon the sauce over the wings, turning them so both sides are covered. Cook until the wings are browned and crispy on the edges, 3 minutes.

Per Serving: Calories 354; Fat 8.11g; Sodium 1340mg; Carbs 15.22g; Fibre 0.2g; Sugar 11.91g; Protein 51.92g

Cajun Chicken and Rice Bowls

Prep time: 10 minutes | **Cook time:** 11 minutes | **Serves:** 4

250 g uncooked long-grain white rice, rinsed
300 ml chicken stock
5 tsp Cajun seasoning
900 g boneless, skinless chicken breast, cut into bite-size pieces
1 red pepper, seeded and chopped

1. Move slider to AIR FRY/STOVETOP. Select SEAR/SAUTÉ and set to Lo1. Select START/STOP to begin preheating. Allow unit to preheat for 5 minutes. Then add the rice to the dry pot, stirring frequently, about 2 minutes. 2. Add the chicken stock, Cajun seasoning, chicken and pepper and stir. Press START/STOP to turn off the SEAR/SAUTÉ function. 3. Close the lid and move slider to PRESSURE. Ensuring the pressure release valve is in the SEAL position. The temperature will default to HIGH, which is the correct setting. Set time to 9 minutes. Select START/STOP to begin cooking. 4. When cooking is complete, release the pressure quickly by turning the pressure release valve to the VENT position. Move slider to the right to unlock the lid, then carefully open it. 5. Season to taste and serve.

Per Serving: Calories 649; Fat 14.24g; Sodium 974mg; Carbs 99.32g; Fibre 4.8g; Sugar 14.39g; Protein 27.41g

Tasty Barbecue Chicken-Stuffed Sweet Potatoes

Prep time: 10 minutes | **Cook time:** 18 minutes | **Serves:** 4

240 g thin barbecue sauce
455 g boneless, skinless chicken thighs, fat trimmed
4 small sweet potatoes, pricked with a fork
Salt and freshly ground black pepper
240 g sour cream
2 green onions, thinly sliced

1. Combine the barbecue sauce and chicken in the pot. 2. Then place the bottom layer of the Deluxe Reversible Rack in the lower position in the pot over the chicken and arrange the sweet potatoes on top. 3. Close the lid and move slider to PRESSURE. Ensuring the pressure release valve is in the SEAL position. The temperature will default to HIGH, which is the correct setting. Set time to 18 minutes. Select START/STOP to begin cooking. 4. When the cooking time is up, let the pressure come down naturally for 10 minutes and then quick-release the remaining pressure. 5. Split the sweet potatoes open lengthwise, season with salt and pepper, and set aside. 6. Remove the rack from the pot. Pull the chicken into shreds with two forks, return it to the sauce, and stir to combine. (The sauce will have browned in places on the bottom of the pot; just scrape them up and stir into the sauce.) 7. Divide the chicken among the sweet potatoes; you may not need all of the sauce. Spread the sour cream on top sprinkle with green onions. Serve.
Per Serving: Calories 468; Fat 13.15g; Sodium 913mg; Carbs 72.99g; Fibre 5g; Sugar 15g; Protein 14.71g

Indian Curried Chicken

Prep time: 10 minutes | **Cook time:** 15 minutes | **Serves:** 4

3 tablespoons butter or ghee, at room temperature
1 medium yellow onion, halved and sliced through the root end
1 (250 g) can tomatoes with green chilies, with juice
2 tablespoons mild Indian curry paste (such as Patak's)
675 g boneless, skinless chicken thighs, fat trimmed, cut into 5 cm to 8cm pieces
2 tablespoons flour
Salt and freshly ground black pepper

1. Add 1 tablespoon of the butter or ghee to the pot, Move slider to AIR FRY/STOVETOP. Select SEAR/SAUTÉ and set to 3. Select START/STOP to begin cooking. Once hot, add onion and cook, stirring often, until browned, 6 minutes. Press START/STOP. 2. Add the tomatoes to the pot, stir, and scrape up any browned bits on the base of the pot. Add the curry paste and stir to combine. Nestle the chicken into the sauce. 3. Close the lid and move slider to PRESSURE, Ensuring the pressure release valve is in the SEAL position. The temperature will default to HIGH, which is the correct setting. Set time to 8 minutes. Select START/STOP to begin cooking. 4. When the cooking time is up, quick-release the pressure. In a small bowl, mix the remaining 2 tablespoons butter or ghee with the flour until smooth. 5. Move slider to AIR FRY/STOVETOP. Select SEAR/SAUTÉ and set to 3. Add the flour mixture to the pot in two additions, Press START/STOP to begin cooking. Stirring between additions, and cook until the sauce is thickened, 1 minute. Press START/STOP. 6. Season with salt and pepper and serve.
Per Serving: Calories 402; Fat 18.43g; Sodium 974mg; Carbs 42.31g; Fibre 2.7g; Sugar 9.96g; Protein 16.84g

Cranberry Hot Chicken Wings

Prep time: 45 minutes | **Cook time:** 35 minutes | **Serves:** 6

- 1 can jellied cranberry sauce
- 120 ml orange juice
- 60 g hot pepper sauce
- 2 tbsp. soy sauce
- 2 tbsp. honey
- 1 tbsp. brown sugar
- 1 tbsp. Dijon mustard
- 2 tsp. garlic powder
- 1 tsp. dried minced onion
- 1 garlic clove, minced
- 24. chicken wings
- 1 tsp. salt
- 4 tsp. cornflour
- 2 tbsp. cold water

1. Whisk together first 10 ingredients. For the chicken, use a sharp knife to cut through two wing joints; discard wing tips. 2. Place wing pieces in the pot; sprinkle with salt. Pour cranberry mixture over top. 3. Close the lid and move slider to PRESSURE. Ensuring the pressure release valve is in the SEAL position. The temperature will default to HIGH, which is the correct setting. Set time to 10 minutes. Select START/STOP to begin cooking. 4. When cooking is complete, release the pressure quickly by turning the pressure release valve to the VENT position. Move slider to the right to unlock the lid, then carefully open it. 5. Remove wings to a plate. Skim fat from cooking juices in the pressure cooker. Place the deluxe reversible rack in the pot in the higher grill position. Place the wings on the rack, then close the lid. 6. Move slider to AIR FRY/STOVETOP. Select GRILL . Press START/STOP to begin cooking, stirring occasionally, until mixture is reduced by half, 20-25 minutes. 7. In a small bowl, mix cornflour and water until smooth; stir into juices. Return to a boil, stirring constantly; cook and stir until glaze is thickened, 1-2 minutes. 8. Grill wings 8 – 10 cm from heat until lightly browned, 2-3 minutes. Brush with glaze before serving. 9. Serve with remaining glaze.
Per Serving: Calories 729; Fat 14.54g; Sodium 966mg; Carbs 61.3g; Fibre 1.1g; Sugar 28.42g; Protein 84.42g

Turkey Verde and Brown Rice

Prep time: 10 minutes | **Cook time:** 22 minutes | **Serves:** 6-8

- 675 g. turkey tenderloins
- 1 tbsp olive oil
- 1 small onion, sliced
- 100 g brown rice, long grain
- 105 g salsa verde
- 240 ml chicken stock
- ½ tsp salt

1. Move slider to AIR FRY/STOVETOP. Select SEAR/SAUTÉ and set to 3. Select START/STOP to begin preheating. Heat the oil and add the onion. Stir and sauté for 3-4 minutes until the onion is translucent. 2. Add the rice, salsa verde, stock , turkey and salt. Stir well. Press START/STOP to reset the cooking program. 3. Close the lid and move slider to PRESSURE. Ensuring the pressure release valve is in the SEAL position. The temperature will default to HIGH, which is the correct setting. Set time to 18 minutes. Select START/STOP to begin cooking. 4. When cooking is complete, naturally release the pressure for 10 minutes. Then release the pressure quickly by turning the pressure release valve to the VENT position. Move slider to AIR FRY/ STOVETOP to unlock the lid, then carefully open it. 5. Transfer the turkey to a plate and slice the meat. Serve with rice.
Per Serving: Calories 599; Fat 48.05g; Sodium 454mg; Carbs 12.49g; Fibre 1g; Sugar 1.14g; Protein 27.26g

Lemony Chicken with Artichoke Avocado

Prep time: 10 minutes | **Cook time:** 15 minutes | **Serves:** 4

2 tbsp extra-virgin olive oil
Juice of ½ lemon
1 tbsp white wine vinegar
Salt
Freshly ground black pepper
4 large boneless, skinless chicken breasts
60 ml white wine
1 can quartered artichoke hearts, drained
1 avocado, peeled, pitted and cubed
1 tsp chopped fresh parsley
Lemon wedges, for serving

1. In a gallon-size resealable plastic bag, combine the olive oil, vinegar, lemon juice, salt, pepper and chicken. 2. Seal the bag and shake to evenly coat the chicken. Marinate the chicken for at least 30 minutes and up to an hour in the refrigerator. 3. Move slider to AIR FRY/STOVETOP. Select SEAR/SAUTÉ and set to 3. Select START/STOP to begin preheating. 4. Place the chicken and its marinade in the pot. Sauté for about 5 minutes on the first side. Flip the chicken, press cancel and then add the white wine. Stir the wine into the marinade. 5. Add the artichoke hearts to the pot. Press START/STOP. 6. Close the lid and move slider to PRESSURE. Ensuring the pressure release valve is in the SEAL position. The temperature will default to HIGH, which is the correct setting. Set time to 10 minutes. Select START/STOP to begin cooking. 7. When cooking is complete, release the pressure quickly by turning the pressure release valve to the VENT position. Move slider to the right to unlock the lid, then carefully open it. 8. Use tongs to transfer the chicken and artichoke hearts to a serving platter. 9. Add the avocado to the platter along with 3 tablespoons of the cooking liquid left in the pot. 10. Top with fresh parsley and add lemon wedges to the platter.
Per Serving: Calories 632; Fat 37.31g; Sodium 519mg; Carbs 10.12g; Fibre 5.7g; Sugar 1.35g; Protein 62.99g

Cheese and Courgette Stuffed Chicken

Prep time: 20 minutes | **Cook time:** 15 minutes | **Serves:** 4

1 slice sturdy sandwich bread, finely chopped
1 small (125 g) courgette, grated
50 g grated Italian cheese blend
1 teaspoon Italian seasoning
Salt and freshly ground black pepper
4 medium boneless, skinless chicken breasts
1 jar thin marinara sauce (such as Rao's)

1. In a medium bowl, combine the breadcrumbs, cheese, courgette, and Italian seasoning. Season with salt and pepper. 2. Cut a horizontal slit into each chicken breast to form a 13 - to 15 cm long pocket. Stuff the chicken breasts with the breadcrumb mixture. Season the chicken with salt and pepper. 3. Pour the sauce into the pot. Add 60 ml water to the marinara jar, screw on the lid, and shake. Add the water to the pot. Place the bottom layer of the Deluxe Reversible Rack in the lower position in the pot and place the chicken breasts on the rack. 4. Close the lid and move slider to PRESSURE, Ensuring the pressure release valve is in the SEAL position. Set the temperature to LOW and set the time to 8 minutes. 5. When the cooking time is up, let the pressure come down naturally for 5 minutes and then quick-release the remaining pressure. 6. Make sure the chicken is cooked through; you should use an instant-read thermometer to check the temperature of the thickest part of the biggest chicken piece, and the thermometer should show a minimum of 75°C. 7. If the chicken isn't done, select SEAR/SAUTÉ and set to Lo1. Remove the rack, nestle the chicken into the sauce, press START/STOP to begin cooking. Simmer a few minutes more, uncovered, until the chicken is done. Press START/STOP. 8. Serve the chicken with the sauce.
Per Serving: Calories 434; Fat 10.02g; Sodium 671mg; Carbs 25.84g; Fibre 1.3g; Sugar 17.98g; Protein 58.38g

Juicy Chicken Sliders

Prep time: 10 minutes | **Cook time:** 30 minutes | **Serves:** 4

2 large boneless, skinless chicken breasts
60 ml water or chicken stock
1 tsp salt
½ tsp ground cumin
¼ tsp freshly ground black pepper
Juice of 1 lime
½ red onion, thinly sliced
1 clove garlic, grated
35 g mild-medium sliced pickled jalapeño peppers
1 tbsp honey
4 brioche slider buns
125 g Gouda cheese, shredded

1. Add the chicken, water or stock, lime juice, salt, cumin, black pepper, red onion, garlic, jalapeños and honey to the pot. 2. Move slider to AIR FRY/STOVETOP. Select SEAR/SAUTÉ and set to 3. Select START/STOP to begin cooking. Once done, press START/STOP to turn off the SEAR/SAUTÉ function. 3. Move slider to PRESSURE, Ensuring the pressure release valve is in the SEAL position. The temperature will default to HIGH, which is the correct setting. Set time to 15 minutes. Select START/STOP to begin cooking. 4. Meanwhile, preheat the oven to 190°C. Line a half sheet pan with foil. Slice the slider buns in half horizontally, placing the bun bottoms on the prepared sheet pan. 5. When cooking is complete, release the pressure quickly by moving the pressure release valve to the VENT position. Move slider to the right to unlock the lid, then carefully open it. 6. Use two forks to shred the chicken and mix together all the contents of the pot. 7. Use tongs to transfer equal amounts of the chicken mixture to each bun bottom. 8. Top each little pile of chicken with a pinch of shredded cheese and then cover with the top bun. 9. Bake the sliders for 15 minutes, or until the cheese melts. Let cool slightly for 2 minutes before serving.

Per Serving: Calories 721; Fat 42.47g; Sodium 1225mg; Carbs 39.55g; Fibre 1.2g; Sugar 22.75g; Protein 44.06g

Smoked Paprika Turkey Lunchmeat

Prep time: 10 minutes | **Cook time:** 20 minutes | **Serves:** 6

1 tbsp smoked paprika
1 tsp coarse salt
1 tsp freshly ground black pepper
1.3 kg turkey breast
240 ml water or chicken stock

1. In a bowl, mix together the paprika, salt and pepper and rub the mixture all over the outside of the turkey breast. 2. Pour the water or chicken stock into the pot. place the bottom layer of the Deluxe Reversible Rack in the lower position in the pot and place the turkey breast on the rack. 3. Close the lid and move slider to PRESSURE. Ensuring the pressure release valve is in the SEAL position. The temperature will default to HIGH, which is the correct setting. Set time to 20 minutes. Select START/STOP to begin cooking. 4. When cooking is complete, release the pressure quickly by turning the pressure release valve to the VENT position. Move slider to the right to unlock the lid, then carefully open it. 5. Remove the turkey breast and place on a carving board. Once cooled enough to handle, thinly slice the turkey and place in an airtight container or resealable plastic bag and store in the refrigerator.

Per Serving: Calories 372; Fat 16.35g; Sodium 597mg; Carbs 2.82g; Fibre 0.6g; Sugar 0.2g; Protein 50.22g

Chicken and Bacon Sandwiches

Prep time: 10 minutes | **Cook time:** 20 minutes | **Serves:** 4

8 slices bacon
½ medium onion, chopped
120 ml chicken stock
900 g boneless, skinless chicken breast
1 (25 g) packet dried ranch seasoning mix
1 (200 g) package cream cheese
100 g shredded cheddar cheese
60 g sour cream
4 buns, split, buttered and toasted
Lettuce, for topping
Sliced tomato, for topping

1. Move slider to AIR FRY/STOVETOP. Select SEAR/SAUTÉ and set to 3. Select START/STOP to begin preheating. 2. Add the bacon. Cook until the bacon is browned and crispy, then remove it with a slotted spoon and place on paper towels to drain any excess fat. Add the onion to the drippings in the pot and cook until starting to soften, 3 to 4 minutes. 3. Add the chicken stock to the pot, taking care to scrape up any browned bits from the bottom of the pot. Then add the chicken, ranch seasoning and cream cheese. Press START/STOP to turn off the SEAR/SAUTÉ function. 4. Close the lid and move slider to PRESSURE. Ensuring the pressure release valve is in the SEAL position. The temperature will default to HIGH, which is the correct setting. Set time to 15 minutes. Select START/STOP to begin cooking. 5. When cooking is complete, release the pressure quickly by moving the pressure release valve to the VENT position. Move slider to the right to unlock the lid, then carefully open it. 6. Carefully shred the chicken. Add the cheddar cheese and sour cream, then stir to combine. 7. Divide the chicken mixture among the buns. Top each with 2 slices of bacon, lettuce and tomato.
Per Serving: Calories 1102; Fat 71.94g; Sodium 1162mg; Carbs 71.31g; Fibre 6.8g; Sugar 17.98g; Protein 42.86g

Cumin Salsa Verde Chicken

Prep time: 10 minutes | **Cook time:** 25 minutes | **Serves:** 6

675 g tomatillos, husks removed
1 large poblano pepper, seeded and sliced in half
2 jalapeño peppers, seeded and sliced in half
1 tbsp olive or avocado oil
80 g diced white onion
20 g fresh coriander, chopped
2 cloves garlic, crushed
Juice of 1 lime
½ tsp sea salt, plus more to taste
900 g boneless chicken thighs
120 ml chicken stock
2 tsp ground cumin
Salt

1. Begin by making the salsa verde: Slice the tomatillos in half and place, cut side down in the pot. 2. Add the peppers, cut side down. Lightly brush with oil. 3. Close the lid and keep slider in the AIR FRY/STOVETOP position. Select BAKE/ROAST, set temperature to 205°C, and set time to 15 minutes. Select START/STOP to begin cooking. 4. Once done, transfer to a plate. 5. In a blender, combine the roasted veggies, onion, coriander, garlic, lime and salt. Pulse and blend until smooth (don't over blend). 6. Place the chicken in the pot. Pour the salsa verde on top. Add the chicken stock and cumin. 7. Close the lid and move slider to PRESSURE. Ensuring the pressure release valve is in the SEAL position. The temperature will default to HIGH, which is the correct setting. Set time to 10 minutes. Select START/STOP to begin cooking. 8. When cooking is complete, release the pressure quickly by turning the pressure release valve to the VENT position. Move slider to the right to unlock the lid, then carefully open it. 9. Shred the chicken with a fork and serve, adding salt to taste.
Per Serving: Calories 437; Fat 30g; Sodium 506mg; Carbs 14.76g; Fibre 3g; Sugar 6.35g; Protein 27.59g

Spiced Mango-Chipotle Shredded Chicken

Prep time: 10 minutes | **Cook time:** 10 minutes | **Serves:** 6

2 tsp smoked paprika
1 tsp ground cumin
½ tsp ground coriander
½ tsp chipotle chili powder
½ tsp sea salt
½ tsp garlic powder
900 g chicken breast
2 mangoes, peeled, pitted and diced
Juice of 1 lime
60 ml coconut aminos
2 tbsp cider vinegar
80 ml water or chicken stock
1 clove garlic, crushed
10 g fresh coriander, chopped
1 tbsp chopped chipotle pepper in adobo sauce
Cooked rice, cauliflower rice or tortillas, for serving
Optional toppings: avocado, onion, mango, fresh coriander, salsa, tomatoes

1. In a small bowl, combine the paprika, chipotle chili powder, cumin, coriander, salt and garlic powder and mix well. Rub all sides of the chicken with the spice mixture. 2. Make the sauce: In a blender or food processor, combine the mangoes, coconut aminos, garlic, vinegar, lime juice, water or stock, coriander and chipotle pepper in adobo sauce. Blend until smooth. 3. Place the chicken in the bottom of the pot. Pour the sauce over the chicken. 4. Close the lid and move slider to PRESSURE. Ensuring the pressure release valve is in the SEAL position. The temperature will default to HIGH, which is the correct setting. Set time to 10 minutes. Select START/STOP to begin cooking. 5. When cooking is complete, naturally release the pressure for 15 minutes. Then release the pressure quickly by turning the pressure release valve to the VENT position. Move slider to AIR FRY/ STOVETOP to unlock the lid, then carefully open it. 6. Then shred the chicken with a knife or fork. 7. Serve over rice or cauliflower rice, or with a tortilla. Add any additional toppings, such as avocado, onion, more mango, coriander, salsa or tomatoes.
Per Serving: Calories 344; Fat 19.3g; Sodium 334mg; Carbs 9.74g; Fibre 3.3g; Sugar 4.89g; Protein 32.88g

Balsamic Mozzarella Chicken Veggie Salad

Prep time: 10 minutes | **Cook time:** 7 minutes | **Serves:** 4

240 ml water or chicken stock
900 g boneless, skinless chicken breast
Coarse salt
180 g spring mix lettuce
150 g cherry tomatoes, halved
15 mini mozzarella balls
1 avocado, peeled, pitted and chopped
60 g balsamic glaze

1. Pour the water or chicken stock into the pot, then add the chicken. 2. Close the lid and move slider to Pressure. Ensuring the pressure release valve is in the SEAL position. The temperature will default to HIGH, which is the correct setting. Set time to 7 minutes. Select START/STOP to begin cooking. 3. When cooking is complete, release the pressure quickly by turning the pressure release valve to the VENT position. Move slider to the right to unlock the lid, then carefully open it. 4. Allow to cool completely, then slice. Season with a little coarse salt. 5. Place the spring mix in a large salad bowl. Top with the sliced chicken, cherry tomatoes, mozzarella balls and avocado. 6. Drizzle with the balsamic glaze and serve immediately.
Per Serving: Calories 825; Fat 38.35g; Sodium 898mg; Carbs 66.81g; Fibre 9.1g; Sugar 20.67g; Protein 52.98g

French Onion Cheese Chicken

Prep time: 15 minutes | **Cook time:** 30 minutes | **Serves:** 6

900 g boneless, skinless chicken breasts, sliced crosswise into fillets about ½ cm thick
65 g flour (by blending a small amount of garlic, onion powder, salt, and black pepper) for dredging
60 ml extra-virgin olive oil
4 tablespoons salted butter, divided
2 Vidalia (sweet) onions, sliced into strands
2 cans non-condensed French onion soup
6–8 slices Texas toast (any variety) or frozen garlic bread
3 tablespoons cornflour
1 packet onion soup/dip mix (optional)
8–10 Swiss cheese slices
Crispy fried onions, for serving (optional)

1. Coat the chicken in the flour mixture and set aside. 2. Place the olive oil and 2 tablespoons of the butter in the pot, move slider to AIR FRY/STOVETOP. Select SEAR/SAUTÉ and set to Hi 5. Select START/STOP to begin preheating, about 3 minutes, until the butter's melted. 3. Working in batches, sear the chicken for 1 minute on each side until very lightly browned, remove the chicken with tongs, and set aside on a plate. Leave any excess oil in the pot for more flavour. 4. Add the remaining 2 tablespoons of butter to the pot and, once melted, add the onions. 5. Sauté for about 10 minutes until they soften and become a bit browned (but not burned), stirring and scraping up any browned bits from the bottom of the pot. Press START/STOP to turn off the SEAR/SAUTÉ function. 6. Add the canned onion soup and stir. Return the chicken to the pot. 7. Close the lid and move slider to PRESSURE. 8. Ensuring the pressure release valve is in the SEAL position. The temperature will default to HIGH, which is the correct setting. Set time to 5 minutes. Select START/STOP to begin cooking. 9. Meanwhile, make the Texas toast (or garlic bread) according to package instructions. When done, line a casserole dish with the toast. 10. When cooking is complete, release the pressure quickly by turning the pressure release valve to the VENT position. Move slider to the right to unlock the lid, then carefully open it. 11. Remove the chicken with tongs and set aside (but leave the sauce in the pot). 12. Still cooking on SEAR/SAUTÉ and set to 3, make the cornflour slurry by mixing the cornflour with 3 tablespoons of water. 13. Add the slurry to the pot along with the onion soup mix (if using) and stir until well combined. 14. Bring to a bubble and cook for about 1 minute, stirring constantly, and then turn off the pot. 15. Let the sauce sit for a few moments until thickened. 16. Layer the chicken over the bread, cover with some of the sauce, place a slice of cheese over it, and add a little more sauce to top it all off. 17. You can pop it into the oven to grill for about 5 minutes so it bubbles and browns. Sprinkle with some crispy fried onions if desired.
Per Serving: Calories 937; Fat 43g; Sodium 1029mg; Carbs 103g; Fibre 8.1g; Sugar 24.77g; Protein 35.75g

Chicken & Dumplings Soup

Prep time: 15 minutes | **Cook time:** 40 minutes | **Serves:** 4-6

The Chicken:
- 4 tablespoons salted butter
- 1 yellow onion, diced
- 2 large carrots, peeled and diced
- 3 ribs celery, sliced into ½ cm pieces, leafy tops reserved
- 3 cloves garlic, minced or pressed
- 1.4 L chicken stock
- 1 whole chicken, chopped into quarters (leg, breast, thigh, and wing; your market's butcher will usually do this for you if you ask nicely)
- 3 bay leaves
- 120 ml cooking sherry
- 1½ teaspoons seasoned salt
- 1½ teaspoons poultry seasoning
- 1½ teaspoons black pepper
- 1½ teaspoons dried sage
- 1 teaspoon dried thyme

The Dumplings:
- 155 g flour, plus more for dusting
- 2 teaspoons baking powder
- 1 teaspoon salt
- 120 ml whole milk
- 2 tablespoons salted butter
- 3 tablespoons cornflour
- 120 g whipping cream or milk

Make the chicken: 1. Place the butter in the pot. Move slider to AIR FRY/STOVETOP. Select SEAR/SAUTÉ and set to Select START/STOP to begin cooking. 2. Once melted, add the carrots, onion, and celery and sauté for 5 minutes, until everything is softened. Add the garlic and sauté for 1 minute longer. 3. Pour in the stock and stir well. Add the chicken and make sure it's all covered by the stock. Toss in the bay leaves. Press START/STOP to turn off the SEAR/SAUTÉ function. 4. Close the lid and move slider to PRESSURE. Ensuring the pressure release valve is in the SEAL position. The temperature will default to HIGH, which is the correct setting. Set time to 10 minutes. Select START/STOP to begin cooking. 5. When cooking is complete, release the pressure quickly by turning the pressure release valve to the VENT position. Move slider to the right to unlock the lid, then carefully open it. 6. Use tongs to remove the chicken from the pot and set aside. Discard the bay leaves. 7. Add the cooking sherry, seasoned salt, sage, pepper, thyme, poultry seasoning, and leafy tops from the celery to the pot and stir well.

Make the dumplings: 1. In a mixing bowl, combine the flour, baking powder, and salt, mix well. 2. Place the milk and butter in a pyrex or other microwave-safe bowl and microwave for 45 seconds, until the butter is completely melted. 3. Pour the milk-butter mixture into the flour and lightly mix with a fork until it comes together into a dough. 4. Use your hands to lightly knead the dough for 1 minute until it's smooth. 5. On a clean surface dusted lightly with flour, use a flour-coated rolling pin to roll the dough to ½ cm thick max. 6. Using a pizza cutter or knife, slice the dough vertically into strips about 2.5 cm-wide and then horizontally about 5 cm apart to make little rectangular strips. 7. Dust with additional flour so they don't stick to each other and gather on a plate. 8. Make a cornflour slurry by combining the cornflour with 3 tablespoons cold water and set aside. 9. Move slider to AIR FRY/STOVETOP. Select SEAR/SAUTÉ and set to Hi 5. Select START/STOP to begin cooking. 10. Once the stock mixture bubbles, immediately stir in the cornflour slurry and add the dumpling strips one by one. 11. Give them a good stir to be sure they aren't sticking together.

Combine the chicken & dumplings: 1. Close the lid and move slider to PRESSURE. Ensuring the pressure release valve is in the SEAL position. The temperature will default to HIGH, which is the correct setting. Set time to 10 minutes. Select START/STOP to begin cooking. 2. In the meantime, pick the chicken meat from the bones, discarding bones, skin, and cartilage. Rip the chicken into pieces by hand. 3. When cooking is complete, release the pressure quickly by turning the pressure release valve to the VENT position. Move slider to the right to unlock the lid, then carefully open it. 4. Add the chicken and whipping cream to the pot and stir until well combined. Allow to cool for 5 minutes and then ladle into bowls.

Per Serving: Calories 984; Fat 37.03g; Sodium 1044mg; Carbs 50.58g; Fibre 3.4g; Sugar 13.45g; Protein 106.66g

Creamy Curry Chicken Bites

Prep time: 5 minutes | **Cook time:** 20 minutes | **Serves:** 4-6

8 tablespoons salted butter
1 large (or 2 medium) yellow onion, diced
6 cloves garlic, minced
½ tablespoon ginger, minced
1.3 kg boneless, skinless chicken thighs, cut into bite-size pieces
1 tablespoon paprika
4 teaspoons garam masala, divided
1 teaspoon ground cumin
½ teaspoon turmeric
1½ teaspoons seasoned salt, divided
½ teaspoon cayenne pepper (optional)
1 can diced tomatoes, with their juices
240 ml unsweetened coconut milk (it should be thin like water and not thick and lumpy)
120 g Greek yogurt
2 tablespoons cornflour
1 (150 g) can tomato paste
120 g whipping cream
Fresh coriander, for serving
Naan, for serving

1. Place the butter in the pot, move slider to AIR FRY/STOVETOP. Select SEAR/SAUTÉ and set to Hi 5. Select START/STOP to begin preheating. 2. Once the butter's melted, add the garlic, onion, and ginger and sauté for 5 minutes, until softened and beginning to brown slightly. 3. Add the chicken and sauté until the edges are pinkish-white in colour, but not yet fully cooked, 2–3 minutes. Add the paprika, turmeric, 3 teaspoons garam masala, cumin, ½ teaspoon seasoned salt, and cayenne (if using) and sauté, stirring, for another minute. 4. Stir in the diced tomatoes and coconut milk and top off with the Greek yogurt, but do not stir in the yogurt! Simply let it rest on top of everything else in the pot. Press START/STOP to turn off the SEAR/SAUTÉ function. 5. Close the lid and move slider to PRESSURE. Ensuring the pressure release valve is in the SEAL position. The temperature will default to HIGH, which is the correct setting. Set time to 8 minutes. Select START/STOP to begin cooking. 6. When cooking is complete, release the pressure quickly by turning the pressure release valve to the VENT position. Move slider to the right to unlock the lid, then carefully open it. 7. In the meantime, mix the cornflour with 2 tablespoons water to form a slurry. Set aside. Stir in the tomato paste, cream, the remaining teaspoon of garam masala, and the remaining teaspoon of seasoned salt. 8. Move slider to AIR FRY/STOVETOP. Select SEAR/SAUTÉ and set to Hi 5. Select START/STOP to begin cooking. 9. Once bubbling, immediately stir in the cornflour slurry and simmer for 30 seconds before hitting Keep Warm/Cancel to turn the pot off. Allow to sit for 5 minutes to thicken. 10. Serve with coriander and naan, if desired.

Per Serving: Calories 812; Fat 37.8g; Sodium 981mg; Carbs 87.17g; Fibre 9.5g; Sugar 26.34g; Protein 32.87g

Marsala Wine Braised Chicken and Mushroom

Prep time: 15 minutes | **Cook time:** 20 minutes | **Serves:** 4-6

- 900 g boneless, skinless chicken breasts, each breast sliced crosswise into fillets about ½ cm thick
- 65 g flour (with a few pinches of garlic powder, black pepper, and salt mixed in) for dredging
- 60 ml extra-virgin olive oil
- 4 tablespoons salted butter, divided
- 1 shallot, minced
- 3 cloves garlic, minced or pressed
- 455 g baby bella mushrooms, sliced
- 180 ml Marsala wine (dry)
- 120 ml chicken stock
- 1½ tablespoons cornflour

1. Coat the chicken in the flour mixture and set aside. 2. Place the olive oil and 1 tablespoon of the butter in the pot. Move slider to AIR FRY/STOVETOP. Select SEAR/SAUTÉ and set to Lo1. Select START/STOP to begin preheating. 3. Once the butter is melted, add the chicken, working in batches, sear the chicken for 1 minute on each side until very lightly browned, remove the chicken with tongs, and set aside on a plate. Leave any excess oil in the pot for more flavour. 4. Melt the remaining 3 tablespoons of butter in the pot—no need to wipe out any oil or flour left behind. 5. Add the shallot and garlic and sauté, scraping up any browned bits from the bottom of the pot, for 2 minutes, then add the mushrooms and sauté for another 2 minutes. 6. Add the wine and give a final scrape to be sure the bottom of the pot is cleared. Add the chicken stock, then put the chicken back in the pot. Press START/STOP. 7. Close the lid and move slider to PRESSURE. Ensuring the pressure release valve is in the SEAL position. The temperature will default to HIGH, which is the correct setting. Set time to 8 minutes. Select START/STOP to begin cooking. Quick release when done. 8. In the meantime, combine the cornflour with 1½ tablespoons cold water to make a slurry. Set aside. 9. Remove the chicken to a serving platter and set aside, but leave the sauce in the pot. Cook on SEAR/SAUTÉ function and set to Hi 5. Once bubbling, immediately stir the cornflour slurry into the sauce. Press START/STOP to stop cooking. 10. Pour the sauce over the chicken and serve.

Per Serving: Calories 785; Fat 23.75g; Sodium 750mg; Carbs 121.26g; Fibre 14.7g; Sugar 12.67g; Protein 33.72g

Chinese-Style Chicken & Broccoli

Prep time: 5 minutes | **Cook time:** 12 minutes | **Serves:** 4-6

5 tablespoons sesame oil
1 tablespoon Shaoxing rice wine (or cooking sherry)
1 bunch of spring onions, thinly sliced
3 cloves garlic, minced or pressed
1 yellow onion, diced
900 g boneless, skinless chicken breasts, cut into bite-size pieces
240 ml beef stock
60 ml hoisin sauce
60 ml low-sodium soy sauce
2 tablespoons oyster sauce
2 tablespoons dark-brown sugar
1–2 heads fresh broccoli, woody end of stalk trimmed and head cut into florets
2 tablespoons cornflour

1. Place the oil and wine in the pot, Move slider to AIR FRY/STOVETOP. Select SEAR/SAUTÉ and set to Lo1. Select START/STOP to begin cooking, 3 minutes. 2. Add the onion and spring onions and cook for 2 minutes, until beginning to soften. Add the garlic and cook for 1 minute more. 3. Add the chicken and cook, stirring, until the edges are pinkish-white in colour, but not yet fully cooked, about 1 minute. Add the beef stock , oyster sauce, hoisin sauce, soy sauce, and brown sugar and stir well to coat. Press START/STOP. 4. Close the lid and move slider to PRESSURE. Ensuring the pressure release valve is in the SEAL position. The temperature will default to HIGH, which is the correct setting. Set time to 4 minutes. Select START/STOP to begin cooking. Quick release when done. 5. Meanwhile, place the broccoli florets in a microwave-safe bowl and pour 60 ml of water over them. Cover loosely with plastic wrap and microwave for 3–4 minutes, until slightly tender but still firm. 6. Mix the cornflour with 2 tablespoons water to form a slurry. Set aside. 7. Once the pot has finished cooking, cook on SEAR/SAUTÉ function again and set to 3. Select START/STOP to begin cooking. 8. When the sauce begins to bubble, immediately add in the cornflour slurry and stir. Stir in the steamed broccoli and allow the liquid to simmer for 30 seconds, until thickened. Press START/STOP to stop cooking. 9. Serve with Hibachi Fried Rice or White or Brown Rice

Per Serving: Calories 522; Fat 25.49g; Sodium 1130mg; Carbs 53.5g; Fibre 3.6g; Sugar 17.21g; Protein 19.43g

Turkey Meatball and Kale Soup with White Beans

Prep time: 10 minutes | **Cook time:** 22 minutes | **Serves:** 6

455 g lean turkey mince
50 g Italian-seasoned dried breadcrumbs
1 large egg white
2 tablespoons olive oil
1 medium yellow onion, chopped
50 g hard salami, chopped
2 medium garlic cloves, peeled and minced (2 teaspoons)
120 g chopped stemmed kale (do not use baby kale)
1.2 L chicken stock
One can white beans, preferably cannellini beans, drained and rinsed
1 teaspoon dried oregano
1 teaspoon dried thyme

1. In a big bowl, combine the turkey mince , breadcrumbs, and egg white, mix well until uniform. Use cleaned and dried hands to form the mixture into 16 balls, each made from about 2 tablespoons of the turkey mince mélange. 2. Move slider to AIR FRY/STOVETOP. Select SEAR/SAUTÉ and set to 3. Select START/STOP to begin preheating. Heat the oil and add the onion, salami, and garlic; cook, stirring frequently, until the onion begins to soften, about 4 minutes. Stir in the kale; continue cooking, stirring more frequently, until the greens wilt, about 3 minutes. 3. Stir in the stock , turn off the SEAR/SAUTÉ function, and scrape up the browned bits on the pot's bottom. Stir in the beans, oregano, and thyme. Add the meatballs and close the lid and move slider to PRESSURE. 4. Ensuring the pressure release valve is in the SEAL position. The temperature will default to HIGH, which is the correct setting. Set time to 15 minutes. Select START/STOP to begin cooking. 5. When cooking is complete, naturally release the pressure for 15 minutes. Then release the pressure quickly by turning the pressure release valve to the VENT position. Move slider to AIR FRY/ STOVETOP to unlock the lid, then carefully open it. 6. Stir gently (to preserve the meatballs) before serving.

Per Serving: Calories 327; Fat 14.75g; Sodium 1025mg; Carbs 23.78g; Fibre 5.4g; Sugar 2.44g; Protein 26.05g

Chapter 5 Seafood Mains Recipes

Rice Pilaf withCorn and Prawns

Prep time: 20 minutes | **Cook time:** 20 minutes | **Serves:** 4

4 tablespoons salted butter
2 large shallots, halved and thinly sliced
¾ teaspoon red pepper flakes
2 teaspoons grated lemon zest, plus 2 teaspoons lemon juice
Salt
300 g long-grain white rice, rinsed and drained
120 g fresh or frozen corn kernels
360 ml low-sodium chicken stock or water
455 g extra-large or large prawns, peeled (tails removed), deveined and chopped into 2 cm pieces
60 g lightly packed baby rocket, roughly chopped
75 g roasted red peppers, patted dry and diced

1. Move slider to AIR FRY/STOVETOP. Select SEAR/SAUTÉ and set to Lo1. Select START/STOP to begin preheating. Add the butter and let melt. 2. Add the shallots, lemon zest, pepper flakes and 1 teaspoon salt, then cook, stirring occasionally, until the shallots are softened, about 3 minutes. 3. add the rice and cook, stirring, until the grains turn translucent, about 2 minutes. add the corn and stock ; stir to combine, then distribute in an even layer, press START/STOP. 4. Close the lid and move slider to PRESSURE. Ensuring the pressure release valve is in the SEAL position. The temperature will default to LOW, which is the correct setting. Set time to 13 minutes. Select START/STOP to begin cooking. 5. When cooking is complete, release the pressure quickly by turning the pressure release valve to the VENT position. Move slider to the right to unlock the lid, then carefully open it. 6. Scatter the prawns in an even layer on the rice, then drape a kitchen towel across the pot and re-cover without locking the lid in place. Let stand for 10 minutes. 7. Stir the prawns into the rice mixture, then re-cover with the towel and lid for another 5 minutes. 8. Fluff the mixture, stirring in the rocket, roasted peppers and lemon juice. 9. Taste and season with salt.

Per Serving: Calories 526; Fat 21.36g; Sodium 864mg; Carbs 76.08g; Fibre 6.1g; Sugar 3.22g; Protein 9.77g

Jollof Rice With Prawns & Peas

Prep time: 30 minutes | **Cook time:** 30 minutes | **Serves:** 4

- 2 tablespoons extra-virgin olive oil
- 1 large yellow onion, chopped
- 2 medium carrots, peeled, halved lengthwise and thinly sliced
- 1 medium red pepper, stemmed, seeded and chopped
- Salt and ground black pepper
- 2 medium garlic cloves, smashed and peeled
- 2 tablespoons curry powder
- 360 g can diced tomatoes
- 300 g basmati rice, rinsed and drained
- 480 ml low-sodium chicken stock
- 1 teaspoon dried thyme
- 300 g extra-large prawns, peeled (tails removed), deveined, halved crosswise and patted dry
- 120 g frozen green peas

1. Move slider to AIR FRY/STOVETOP. Select SEAR/SAUTÉ and set to Hi 5. Select START/STOP to begin preheating. Add the oil and heat until shimmering. 2. Add the onion, carrots, pepper and 1 teaspoon salt, then cook, stirring, until the onion is softened and golden brown at the edges, 5 to 7 minutes. 3. Stir in the garlic and curry powder, then cook until fragrant, about 30 seconds. 4. Add the tomatoes with their juices, the rice, stock and thyme; stir to combine then distribute in an even layer, press START/STOP. 5. Close the lid and move slider to PRESSURE. Ensuring the pressure release valve is in the SEAL position. The temperature will default to LOW, which is the correct setting. Set time to 10 minutes. Select START/STOP to begin cooking. 6. In the meantime, season the prawns with salt and black pepper; set aside. 7. When pressure-cooking is complete, quick-release the steam by moving the pressure valve to Vent. Press START/STOP, then carefully open the pot. 8. Scatter the prawns and peas evenly on the rice, then re-cover without locking the lid in place. 9. Let stand until the prawns are opaque throughout, about 10 minutes. 10. Fluff the rice, stirring in the prawns and peas. Taste and season with salt and pepper.

Per Serving: Calories 382; Fat 25.34g; Sodium 885mg; Carbs 43.9g; Fibre 18.4g; Sugar 7.8g; Protein 12.91g

Garlicky Salmon

Prep time: 10 minutes | **Cook time:** 12 minutes | **Serves:** 2-4

½ tsp salt
¼ tsp garlic powder
¼ tsp onion powder
¼ tsp dried chives
¼ tsp freshly ground black pepper
2 (300 g) salmon fillets
1 tbsp olive oil
1 tbsp unsalted butter
Juice of ½ lemon
1 tbsp white wine
1½ tsp chopped fresh dill
1½ tsp chopped fresh parsley

1. In a small bowl, combine the salt, onion powder, garlic powder, chives and pepper. Season each salmon fillet liberally with the mixture. 2. Move slider to AIR FRY/STOVETOP. Select SEAR/SAUTÉ and set to Lo1. Select START/STOP to begin preheating. 3. Add the oil and butter to the preheated pot. Add the salmon fillets, skin side down. Sauté for 7 to 9 minutes, or until the skin is nice and crispy. Press START/STOP. 4. Carefully remove the salmon with a fish spatula. Some parts of the skin might stick; work carefully so as to not break the fish. Transfer the fish to a large plate. 5. Deglaze the pot with the lemon juice and white wine. Scrape up any browned bits from the bottom of the pot. 6. Then place the bottom layer of the Deluxe Reversible Rack in the lower position in the pot. 7. Place the fillets on the rack. Close the lid and move slider to PRESSURE. Ensuring the pressure release valve is in the SEAL position. The temperature will default to HIGH, which is the correct setting. Set time to 3 minutes. Select START/STOP to begin cooking. 8. When the cooking is complete, quick release the pressure. 9. Remove the lid and carefully transfer each fillet to a serving plate. 10. Spoon some of the sauce from the pot over each fish, then top with fresh dill and parsley.

Per Serving: Calories 244; Fat 15.39g; Sodium 882mg; Carbs 1.72g; Fibre 0.4g; Sugar 0.28g; Protein 23.88g

Delicious Prawns Stew with White Beans & Spinach

Prep time: 10 minutes | **Cook time:** 15 minutes | **Serves:** 4

2 tablespoons olive oil
1 medium yellow onion, chopped
3 medium garlic cloves, peeled and minced
1 tablespoon loosely packed fresh rosemary leaves, minced
½ teaspoon red pepper flakes (optional)
720 ml chicken stock
300 g can white beans, drained and rinsed
455 g medium prawns, peeled and deveined
120 g packed, chopped, and stemmed spinach leaves
2 tablespoons fresh lemon juice
½ teaspoon salt
½ teaspoon ground black pepper

1. Move slider to AIR FRY/STOVETOP. Select SEAR/SAUTÉ and set to 3. Select START/STOP to begin preheating. Heat the oil for 1-2 minute and add the onion and cook, stirring occasionally, until softened, about 4 minutes. Stir in the garlic, rosemary, and red pepper flakes (if using) until aromatic, just a few seconds. 2. Pour in the stock and scrape up any browned bits on the pot's bottom. Press START/STOP to turn off the SEAR/SAUTÉ function. 3. Add the beans, and stir well. Close the lid and move slider to PRESSURE. Ensuring the pressure release valve is in the SEAL position. The temperature will default to HIGH, which is the correct setting. Set time to 3 minutes. Select START/STOP to begin cooking. 4. When cooking is complete, release the pressure quickly by turning the pressure release valve to the VENT position. Move slider to the right to unlock the lid, then carefully open it. 5. Select the SEAR/SAUTÉ function again and set to 3. Bring the sauce to a simmer, stirring occasionally. Add the prawns and spinach. Stir well, then set the lid askew over the pot and cook for 1 minute. 6. Turn off the SEAR/SAUTÉ function and stir in the lemon juice, salt, and pepper. 7. Set the lid askew again over the pot and set aside for 3 minutes to blend the flavours and further cook the prawns. Serve hot in bowls.

Per Serving: Calories 643; Fat 21.9g; Sodium 1072mg; Carbs 41.36g; Fibre 12.6g; Sugar 3.17g; Protein 71.4g

Lime Prawns & Corn Salad

Prep time: 10 minutes | **Cook time:** 2 minutes | **Serves:** 4

Juice and zest of 1 lime
1 tsp soy sauce or coconut aminos
1 tbsp chili powder
2 cloves garlic, minced
1 jalapeño pepper, seeded and minced
½ tsp ground cumin
1 tsp smoked paprika
¼ tsp freshly ground black pepper, plus more to taste
Dressing:
2 tbsp light sour cream
1 tbsp fresh lime juice
1 tsp sauce from the pot

½ tsp salt, plus more to taste
2 tbsp hot sauce, such as Valentina
455 g frozen and thawed deveined prawns
2 ears corn, husked
1 head romaine lettuce, chopped
40 g shredded purple cabbage
135 g Pico de Gallo

Salt
Freshly ground black pepper

1. Add the lime juice and zest, soy sauce, chili powder, garlic, jalapeño, cumin, paprika, salt, black pepper and hot sauce to the pot, stir to mix well. Add the prawns and mix until evenly coated. 2. Then place the bottom layer of the Deluxe Reversible Rack in the lower position in the pot. 3. Place the ears of corn on the rack. Close the lid and move slider to PRESSURE. Ensuring the pressure release valve is in the SEAL position. The temperature will default to HIGH, which is the correct setting. Set time to 2 minutes. Select START/STOP to begin cooking. 4. When the time is up, quick release the pressure. Use tongs to remove the ears of corn and transfer them to a cutting board. Stand an ear on one end. Use a knife to slice along each cob to remove the kernels from the cob. 5. To assemble the salad, place the lettuce and then cabbage on the bottom of a large bowl. Top with the Pico de Gallo, corn kernels and prawns. 6. To prepare the dressing, in a separate bowl, whisk together the sour cream, lime juice, cooking liquid from the pot and salt and pepper to taste. 7. Dress the salad with the dressing. Add more salt and pepper to taste, if desired.

Per Serving: Calories 287; Fat 7.37g; Sodium 863mg; Carbs 53.34g; Fibre 7.1g; Sugar 31.34g; Protein 9.22g

Creamy Seafood and Noodles Casserole

Prep time: 10 minutes | **Cook time:** 10 minutes | **Serves:** 6

600 ml chicken stock
120 ml dry sherry
2 tablespoons butter
1 tablespoon fresh minced tarragon leaves
½ teaspoon mild paprika
¼ teaspoon table salt
300 g wide egg or no-yolk noodles
180 g whipping cream
1 large egg yolk
225 g sea scallops, quartered
225 g small prawns, peeled, deveined, and cut in half lengthwise

1. Move slider to AIR FRY/STOVETOP. Select SEAR/SAUTÉ and set to 3. Select START/STOP to begin preheating. 2. Add the stock, sherry, paprika, butter, tarragon, and salt to the pot. Cook until the butter melts, stirring occasionally, about 3 minutes. 3. Press START/STOP to turn off the SEAR/SAUTÉ function and stir in the noodles until coated. 4. Close the lid and move slider to PRESSURE. Ensuring the pressure release valve is in the SEAL position. The temperature will default to HIGH, which is the correct setting. Set time to 3 minutes. Select START/STOP to begin cooking. 5. When cooking is complete, release the pressure quickly by turning the pressure release valve to the VENT position. Move slider to the right to unlock the lid, then carefully open it. 6. Then Move slider to AIR FRY/STOVETOP. Select SEAR/SAUTÉ and set to Lo1. Select START/STOP to begin cooking. 7. Whisk the cream and egg yolk in a small bowl. Whisk some of the hot mixture from the pot into this cream mixture, then stir this combined mixture back into the pot along with the scallops and prawns. 8. Cook, stirring frequently, just until the prawns are firm, not more than 2 minutes. Press START/STOP to turn off the SEAR/SAUTÉ function. 9. Remove the hot insert from the pot to stop the cooking, and continue stirring until any bubbling stops and the noodles are well coated.
Per Serving: Calories 445; Fat 25.64g; Sodium 1102mg; Carbs 9.48g; Fibre 0.7g; Sugar 5.08g; Protein 42.74g

Curried Prawns with Vegetables & Rice Vermicelli

Prep time: 10 minutes | **Cook time:** 5 minutes | **Serves:** 6

720 ml chicken stock
6 tablespoons soy sauce
2 tablespoons unseasoned rice vinegar
1 tablespoon yellow curry powder
1 tablespoon sambal oelek
200 g dried rice vermicelli
335 g small prawns. peeled and deveined
455 g mixed frozen vegetables for stir-fry, any seasoning packets discarded (do not thaw)

1. Add the stock, soy sauce, curry powder, rice vinegar, and sambal oelek to the pot. Break the vermicelli to fit in the pot and set them in the sauce. 2. Lay the prawns over the noodles and sauce, then pour the frozen mixed vegetables in an even layer on top. 3. Close the lid and move slider to PRESSURE. Ensuring the pressure release valve is in the SEAL position. The temperature will default to HIGH, which is the correct setting. Set time to 5 minutes. Select START/STOP to begin cooking. 4. When cooking is complete, naturally release the pressure for 3 minutes. Then release the pressure quickly by turning the pressure release valve to the VENT position. 5. Move slider to AIR FRY/ STOVETOP to unlock the lid, then carefully open it. Stir well before serving.
Per Serving: Calories 404; Fat 14.2g; Sodium 1324mg; Carbs 50.66g; Fibre 3.5g; Sugar 14.08g; Protein 18.41g

Lemny Salmon with Horseradish Sauce

Prep time: 15 minutes | **Cook time:** 5 minutes | **Serves:** 6

1.2 L vegetable stock
240 ml dry white wine, such as Chardonnay
1 small lemon, scrubbed to remove any waxy coating, then thinly sliced and seeded
4 or 5 fresh dill fronds
1 teaspoon black peppercorns
1 bay leaf
One 900 g skin-on salmon fillet
120 g regular or low-fat mayonnaise
120 g regular or low-fat sour cream
2 tablespoons fresh lemon juice
2 tablespoons minced dill fronds
2 tablespoons jarred prepared white horseradish
1 tablespoon minced chives or spring onion (green part only)
½ teaspoon ground black pepper

1. Add the stock, wine, peppercorns, lemon, dill, and bay leaf to the pot. Set the salmon skin side down in the stock mixture. Close the lid and move slider to PRESSURE. Ensuring the pressure release valve is in the SEAL position. The temperature will default to LOW, which is the correct setting. Set time to 4 minutes. Select START/STOP to begin cooking. 2. When cooking is complete, release the pressure quickly by turning the pressure release valve to the VENT position. Move slider to the right to unlock the lid, then carefully open it. Set aside and cool for 1 hour. 3. In the meantime, whisk the mayonnaise, sour cream, horseradish, lemon juice, dill, chives, and pepper in a small bowl until smooth. Cover and refrigerate until you're ready to serve. 4. After an hour, transfer the salmon to a platter. Discard the liquid and solids in the pot. 5. Slice the fish and serve at once—or cover and refrigerate for up to 2 days, offering the horseradish sauce on the side.

Per Serving: Calories 430; Fat 17.3g; Sodium 1483mg; Carbs 19.12g; Fibre 3.2g; Sugar 4.07g; Protein 51.72g

Herbed Clams

Prep time: 10 minutes | **Cook time:** 4 minutes | **Serves:** 4

240 ml liquid (Choose one or two from wine of any sort, beer of any sort, stock of any sort, sherry, vermouth, and/or unsweetened apple juice)
2 tablespoons liquid or solid fat (Choose from butter, rendered bacon fat, coconut oil, or lard—or olive, vegetable, corn, rapeseed, safflower, or any nut oil)
2 tablespoons acid (Choose from vinegar of any sort, lemon juice, or lime juice)
2 tablespoons minced fresh herb leaves (Choose one or preferably two from basil, coriander, marjoram, parsley, oregano, sage, savory, tarragon, and/or thyme)
3 medium garlic cloves, peeled and minced (1 tablespoon—optional)
1.3 kg small littleneck, mahogany, or manila clams, scrubbed

1. Add the liquid, fat, acid, herbs, and garlic (if using) to the pot and mix well. Stir in the clams. Close the lid and move slider to PRESSURE. Ensuring the pressure release valve is in the SEAL position. The temperature will default to HIGH, which is the correct setting. Set time to 4 minutes. Select START/STOP to begin cooking. 2. When cooking is complete, naturally release the pressure for 15 minutes. Then release the pressure quickly by turning the pressure release valve to the VENT position. Move slider to AIR FRY/ STOVETOP to unlock the lid, then carefully open it. 3. Spoon the clams into bowls. (Discard any that do not open.) Ladle lots of the sauce from the pot over them in the bowls.

Per Serving: Calories 260; Fat 7.81g; Sodium 1235mg; Carbs 45.82g; Fibre 1.7g; Sugar 17.44g; Protein 2.34g

Seafood and Veggie Stew

Prep time: 10 minutes | **Cook time:** 25 minutes | **Serves:** 6

360 ml water
900 g Manila or small cherrystone clams, scrubbed for sand
2 tablespoons butter
2 tablespoons olive oil
1 medium yellow onion, chopped
1 small fennel bulb (about 150 g), trimmed and chopped
2 medium celery stalks, thinly sliced
1 medium carrot, chopped
1 small green pepper, stemmed, seeded, and chopped
3 medium garlic cloves, peeled and minced (1 tablespoon)
One 700 g can crushed tomatoes
480 ml chicken stock
20 g loosely packed fresh parsley leaves, finely chopped
2 tablespoons tomato paste
1 tablespoon Worcestershire sauce
1 teaspoon dried oregano
1 teaspoon dried thyme
½ teaspoon ground black pepper
225 g thick-fleshed, skinless fish fillets, such as cod or halibut, cut into 2.5 cm pieces
225 g medium prawns, peeled and deveined
225 g small sea scallops, halved
Red pepper flakes for garnishing (optional)

1. Pour the water into the pot. Add the clams to the pot. 2. Close the lid and move slider to PRESSURE. Ensuring the pressure release valve is in the SEAL position. The temperature will default to HIGH, which is the correct setting. Set time to 2 minutes. Select START/STOP to begin cooking. 3. When cooking is complete, release the pressure quickly by turning the pressure release valve to the VENT position. Move slider to the right to unlock the lid, then carefully open it. 4. Use a slotted spoon to transfer the clams to a large bowl. Discard any clams that do not open. 5. Strain the liquid in the pot through a fine-mesh sieve like a chinois (or a colander lined with a double layer of cheesecloth) into a bowl below. Rinse out the pot and return it to the machine. 6. Move slider to AIR FRY/STOVETOP. Select SEAR/SAUTÉ and set to 3. Select START/STOP to begin cooking. Melt the butter in the oil, then add the onion, fennel, celery, carrot, pepper, and garlic. Cook, stirring frequently, until the onion softens and the vegetables are fragrant, about 6 minutes. 7. Stir in the tomatoes, stock, and the reserved, strained clam cooking water. Scrape up any browned bits on the pot's bottom and turn off the SEAR/SAUTÉ function. 8. Stir in the parsley, oregano, tomato paste, Worcestershire sauce, thyme, and pepper until the tomato paste dissolves. 9. Close the lid and move slider to PRESSURE. Ensuring the pressure release valve is in the SEAL position. The temperature will default to HIGH, which is the correct setting. Set time to 5 minutes. Select START/STOP to begin cooking. 10. When cooking is complete, release the pressure quickly by turning the pressure release valve to the VENT position. Move slider to the right to unlock the lid, then carefully open it. Stir well. Add the fish, prawns, and scallops. 11. Move slider to AIR FRY/STOVETOP. Select SEAR/SAUTÉ and set to 3. Select START/STOP to begin cooking. Stir gently, then cook, stirring very carefully, until the prawns are pink and firm, about 4 minutes. 12. Turn off the START/STOP function and gently stir the reserved clams into the sauce. 13. Set the lid askew over the pot and set aside for 5 minutes to warm the clams and blend the flavours. 14. Serve in big bowls with red pepper flakes on the side, if desired.

Per Serving: Calories 418; Fat 15.39g; Sodium 1321mg; Carbs 37.07g; Fibre 6g; Sugar 15.67g; Protein 34g

Herbed Crab Cake

Prep time: 30 minutes | **Cook time:** 20 minutes | **Serves:** 6

2 tablespoons olive oil, plus additional for greasing the pan	120 g regular or low-fat mayonnaise
2 medium celery stalks, thinly sliced	1 large egg
1 small yellow onion, chopped	2 tablespoons Dijon mustard
1 small yellow pepper, stemmed, cored, and chopped	1 tablespoon dried sage
360 ml water	1 teaspoon ground black pepper
1 teaspoon mild paprika	½ teaspoon dried thyme
110 g plain panko breadcrumbs	Several dashes hot red pepper sauce,
	455 g crabmeat, picked over for shells and cartilage

1. Move slider to AIR FRY/STOVETOP. Select SEAR/SAUTÉ and set to 3. Select START/STOP to begin preheating. 2. Heat the oil in the pot for 1-2 minutes. Add the celery, onion, and pepper. Cook, stirring occasionally, until the onion softens, about 3 minutes. 3. Scrape this mixture into a large bowl and set aside to cool to room temperature, about 20 minutes. In the meantime, clean and dry the insert; return it to the pot. 4. Pour the water into the pot. Then place the bottom layer of the Deluxe Reversible Rack in the lower position in the pot. 5. Generously oil the inside of the multi-purpose pan. Sprinkle the paprika evenly around the interior of the pan, giving it a light coating. 6. Stir the breadcrumbs, mayonnaise, mustard, sage, egg white, thyme, pepper, and hot red pepper sauce (if using) into the onion mixture until uniform. 7. Gently stir in the crabmeat, then pack this mixture into the prepared pan. Cover the pan tightly with foil, then use a knife to poke a large hole in the centre of the foil where the centre hole of the pan is. 8. Transfer the pan to the rack in the cooker. Close the lid, making sure the lid seals tight without any foil sticking out around the rim. 9. Move slider to PRESSURE and Ensuring the pressure release valve is in the SEAL position. The temperature will default to HIGH, which is the correct setting. Set time to 15 minutes. Select START/STOP to begin cooking. 10. When cooking is complete, naturally release the pressure for 20 minutes. Then release the pressure quickly by turning the pressure release valve to the VENT position. Move slider to AIR FRY/ STOVETOP to unlock the lid, then carefully open it. 11. Transfer the hot pan to a wire cooling rack. Cool for 15 minutes, then set a plate over the pan, invert the whole thing, and remove the pan. 12. Cool for another 5 minutes or so before slicing into wedges to serve.

Per Serving: Calories 454; Fat 34.17g; Sodium 309mg; Carbs 12.63g; Fibre 5.5g; Sugar 3.48g; Protein 29.7g

Prawns and Potatoes with Cocktail Sauce

Prep time: 10 minutes | **Cook time:** 7 minutes | **Serves:** 4

900 g shell-on small prawns, deveined
675 g small red-skinned potatoes, each slightly smaller than a Ping-Pong ball, halved
2 tablespoons olive oil
Up to 2 tablespoons Old Bay seasoning or other fish boil seasoning
480 ml water
240 g red chili sauce, such as Heinz chili sauce
2 tablespoons fresh lemon juice
1 tablespoon prepared jarred white horseradish
1 tablespoon minced fresh dill fronds
Several dashes hot red pepper sauce, such as Tabasco Sauce

1. In a large bowl, mix together the prawns, potatoes, olive oil, and seasoning, toss until the prawns and potatoes are evenly and thoroughly coated. 2. Pour the water into the pot. Then place the bottom layer of the Deluxe Reversible Rack in the lower position in the pot. Place the prawns and potatoes on the rack. 3. Close the lid and move slider to PRESSURE. Ensuring the pressure release valve is in the SEAL position. The temperature will default to HIGH, which is the correct setting. Set time to 7 minutes. Select START/STOP to begin cooking. 4. In the meantime, make the cocktail sauce. Whisk the chili sauce, lemon juice, horseradish, dill, and hot red pepper sauce in a small serving bowl. Set aside. 5. When cooking is complete, naturally release the pressure for 10 minutes. Then release the pressure quickly by turning the pressure release valve to the VENT position. Move slider to AIR FRY/STOVETOP to unlock the lid, then carefully open it. 6. Lift the hot rack out of the pot and pour the prawns and potatoes onto a serving plate. Serve with the cocktail sauce on the side.
Per Serving: Calories 365; Fat 10.03g; Sodium 1349mg; Carbs 34.18g; Fibre 4.1g; Sugar 4.34g; Protein 35.07g

Garlicky Buttery Prawns

Prep time: 10 minutes | **Cook time:** 7 minutes | **Serves:** 6-8

720 ml chicken stock or fish stock
240 ml beer, preferably an amber ale
115 g butter, cut into chunks
80 g tomato paste
6 medium garlic cloves, peeled and minced (2 tablespoons)
2 teaspoons dried thyme
1 teaspoon dried oregano
1 teaspoon fennel seeds
1 teaspoon red pepper flakes
½ teaspoon table salt
½ teaspoon celery seeds (optional)
1.3 kg large prawns, peeled and deveined
Crunchy bread, for serving

1. Combine the stock, beer, tomato paste, oregano, garlic, butter, thyme, fennel seeds, salt, red pepper flakes, and celery seed (if using) in the pot and close the lid. 2. Move slider to PRESSURE. Ensuring the pressure release valve is in the SEAL position. The temperature will default to HIGH, which is the correct setting. Set time to 5 minutes. Select START/STOP to begin cooking. 3. When cooking is complete, release the pressure quickly by turning the pressure release valve to the VENT position. 4. Move slider to the right to unlock the lid, then carefully open it. Then move the slider to AIR FRY/STOVETOP. Select SEAR/SAUTÉ and set to 3. Stir the sauce as it comes to a simmer. 5. Add the prawns, stir well, and set the lid askew over the pot. Select START/STOP to begin cooking. 6. Cook until the prawns are pink and firm, about 2 minutes. Turn off the SEAR/SAUTÉ function to stop the cooking. 7. Set aside to cool, pour the contents of the pot into a large serving bowl and serve with the crunchy bread to sop up the sauce.
Per Serving: Calories 400; Fat 22.14g; Sodium 1786mg; Carbs 17.64g; Fibre 2.5g; Sugar 5.31g; Protein 32.46g

Creamy Seafood Chowder

Prep time: 20 minutes | **Cook time:** 15 minutes | **Serves:** 6

- 455 g large prawns
- 1.5 L chicken stock
- 2 medium carrots, thinly sliced
- 3 medium celery stalks, thinly sliced
- 1 medium yellow onion, chopped
- 2 small yellow potatoes, such as Yukon Golds, chopped
- 70 g fresh or frozen corn kernels (no need to thaw)
- 2 medium garlic cloves, peeled and minced
- 2 tablespoons tomato paste
- 1 tablespoon stemmed fresh thyme leaves
- ¼ teaspoon table salt
- 225 g pasteurized claw or "special" crabmeat, picked over for shell and cartilage
- 225 g sea scallops, quartered
- 225 g thin skinless white fish fillets, such as fluke, haddock, hake, or snapper, cut into 2.5 cm pieces
- 120 g whipping cream

1. Peel and devein the prawns, discard the veins. Place the shells in the pot. Pour the stock into the pot, stir well, and close the lid onto the pot. Move slider to PRESSURE and Ensuring the pressure release valve is in the SEAL position. The temperature will default to HIGH, which is the correct setting. Set time to 3 minutes. Select START/STOP to begin cooking. 2. When cooking is complete, release the pressure quickly by turning the pressure release valve to the VENT position. Move slider to the right to unlock the lid, then carefully open it. 3. Use a slotted spoon to fish out and discard all the prawns shells, as well as any extraneous bits. 4. Stir in the carrots, celery, tomato paste, thyme, potatoes, corn, onion, garlic, and salt until the tomato paste dissolves. 5. Close the lid. Move slider to AIR FRY/STOVETOP. Select SEAR/SAUTÉ and set to 3. Select START/STOP to begin cooking. 6. Bring the soup to a simmer, stirring occasionally. Stir in the peeled prawns, crabmeat, scallops, and fish. 7. Continue cooking just until the prawns are barely pink, 2 to 3 minutes. Press START/STOP to turn off the SEAR/SAUTÉ function, stir in the cream, and set the lid over the pot for 5 minutes to blend the flavours.

Per Serving: Calories 343; Fat 7.19g; Sodium 1703mg; Carbs 38.99g; Fibre 4.1g; Sugar 10.09g; Protein 31.81g

Chapter 6 Beef, Pork and Lamb Recipes

Beef and Carrot Stew with Bacon

Prep time: 10 minutes | **Cook time:** 40 minutes | **Serves:** 6

5 strips bacon, roughly chopped
1.3 kg beef chuck, fat trimmed, cut into 5 cm chunks
Salt and freshly ground black pepper
1 large yellow onion, chopped
Optional Add-ins:
5 (8 cm) sprigs fresh thyme, or 1 (8 cm) sprig rosemary
120 ml Pinot Noir
3 large carrots, peeled and cut into 1 cm-thick coins
180 ml store-bought beef stock, or homemade
30 g flour
2 tablespoons tomato paste

1. Place the bacon in the pot, move slider to AIR FRY/STOVETOP. Select SEAR/SAUTÉ and set to 3. Select START/STOP to begin cooking, stirring frequently, until the bacon is browned and crisp, 3 to 4 minutes. Press START/STOP. 2. Transfer the bacon to a paper towel–lined plate. Spoon off all but 1½ tablespoons of the drippings in the pot and discard. 3. Season the beef with ¾ teaspoon salt and several grinds of pepper. 4. Select SEAR/SAUTÉ function and set to Hi 5. Add one handful of the meat (6 or 7 pieces) to the pot. Do not overcrowd; there should be space between the pieces of meat so they will brown. Press START/STOP to begin cooking. 5. Cook without stirring until well browned on one side, 3 minutes. Stir and cook for a few minutes more. 6. Add the onion and cook, stirring frequently, until the onion is becoming tender, 3 minutes. 7. Add the wine and simmer for 2 minutes, scraping up the browned bits on the bottom of the pot. Press START/STOP to stop cooking. 8. Add the remaining beef, carrots, bacon, 120 ml of the stock, and the optional add-ins (if using). 9. Close the lid, move slider to PRESSURE, Ensuring the pressure release valve is in the SEAL position. The temperature will default to HIGH, which is the correct setting. Set time to 25 minutes. Select START/STOP to begin cooking. 10. When the cooking time is up, let the pressure come down naturally for 10 minutes and then quick-release the remaining pressure. 11. Discard the herb sprigs, if you used them. 12. Place the flour in a small bowl and gradually whisk in the remaining 60 ml stock. Add the flour mixture to the pot, cook on SEAR/SAUTÉ function and set to 3, and simmer, gently stirring occasionally, until thickened and bubbly, 2 minutes. 13. Season with salt and pepper and serve.

Per Serving: Calories 399; Fat 15.94g; Sodium 423mg; Carbs 12.89g; Fibre 1.8g; Sugar 3.01g; Protein 48.42g

Homemade Beef & Beets Borscht

Prep time: 15 minutes | **Cook time:** 20 minutes | **Serves:** 4

1 large bunch red beets with greens
600 g beef chuck roast, trimmed and cut into 1 cm chunks
1 tablespoon extra-virgin olive oil
Salt and freshly ground black pepper
600 ml store-bought beef stock, or homemade
Optional Garnish:
180 g sour cream or plain Greek yogurt
1 yellow onion, chopped
1 teaspoon caraway seeds
1 teaspoon dried dill
1 tablespoon balsamic or red wine vinegar

1. Wash the beets and the greens well. Peel the beets and cut them into 1 cm pieces; set aside. Finely chop the stems and greens (keep them separate); set aside. 2. Toss half the beef with the oil and season generously with salt and pepper. 3. Move slider to AIR FRY/STOVETOP. Select SEAR/SAUTÉ and set to Hi 5. Select START/STOP to begin preheating. When the pot is hot, add the seasoned beef and cook, stirring occasionally, until well browned, 4 minutes. Press START/STOP. 4. Add the remaining (unbrowned) beef, the stock, onions, beets, beet stems, caraway, and dill to the pot. (You'll add the beet greens at the end of cooking.) 5. Close the lid and move slider to PRESSURE. Ensuring the pressure release valve is in the SEAL position. The temperature will default to HIGH, which is the correct setting. Set time to 15 minutes. Select START/STOP to begin cooking. 6. When cooking is complete, naturally release the pressure for 10 minutes. Then release the pressure quickly by turning the pressure release valve to the VENT position. Move slider to AIR FRY/ STOVETOP to unlock the lid, then carefully open it. 7. Add the vinegar and beet greens to the pot. Cook on SEAR/SAUTÉ function and set to Hi 5. Cook until the soup is simmering and the greens are tender, 1 minute. Press START/STOP. 8. Season with salt and pepper. Garnish with the sour cream, if desired.

Per Serving: Calories 479; Fat 22.3g; Sodium 668mg; Carbs 27.39g; Fibre 2.3g; Sugar 7.9g; Protein 42.3g

Beef Sandwiches with Cheese Sauce

Prep time: 10 minutes | **Cook time:** 50 minutes | **Serves:** 4

2 tsp olive oil
1 (900 g) chuck roast
Coarse salt
Freshly ground black pepper
1 medium onion, sliced

240 ml beef stock
30 g plain flour
480 ml whole milk
100 g shredded smoked Gouda cheese
1 loaf crusty bread, sliced and toasted

1. Move slider to AIR FRY/STOVETOP. Select SEAR/SAUTÉ and set to 3. Select START/STOP to begin preheating. 2. When the pot is hot, add the oil to the pot. Season your chuck roast well with salt and pepper, then add the roast to the pot and brown it well on all sides. Remove the roast and set aside. 3. Add the onion to the drippings in the pot and scrape up any browned bits on the bottom of the pot. Sauté the onion until it is soft and starting to caramelize, about 10 minutes. Press START/STOP to turn off the SEAR/SAUTÉ function. 4. Add the beef stock, taking care to scrape up any browned bits from the base of the pot. Place the roast directly into the liquid. 5. Close the lid and move slider to PRESSURE. Ensuring the pressure release valve is in the SEAL position. The temperature will default to HIGH, which is the correct setting. Set time to 40 minutes. Select START/STOP to begin cooking. 6. In the meantime, in a small saucepan, whisk together the flour and milk to make a sauce. 7. Cook over medium heat until it starts to thicken, about 3 to 4 minutes. Add the shredded cheese, 1 small handful at a time, gently stirring to incorporate before adding more. Season well with salt and pepper. 8. When the cooking is complete, quick release the pressure and carefully remove the lid. Using two forks to shred the meat with and stir the meat into the liquid in the pot. 9. Divide the meat mixture among the toasted slices of bread. Drizzle with the cheese sauce and serve.
Per Serving: Calories 548; Fat 22.52g; Sodium 1119mg; Carbs 28.29g; Fibre 0.5g; Sugar 17.79g; Protein 55.58g

Pulled Pork and Pineapple Sandwiches

Prep time: 10 minutes | **Cook time:** 55 minutes | **Serves:** 8

2 tbsp olive oil
1 tsp ground cinnamon
2 tsp allspice
1 tsp coarse salt
1 tsp freshly ground black pepper
¼ tsp freshly ground nutmeg

2 tsp dried thyme
½ tsp cayenne pepper
1 (1.6 kg) pork shoulder
240 ml water or chicken stock
Crusty rolls
Sliced pineapple

1. Combine the olive oil, cinnamon, salt, black pepper, allspice, nutmeg, thyme and cayenne in a small bowl. Rub the mixture all over the pork roast. 2. Move slider to AIR FRY/STOVETOP. Select SEAR/SAUTÉ and set to 3. Select START/STOP to begin preheating. 3. Add the roast to the preheated pot and brown it well on all sides, adding a little oil to the pot, if necessary. 4. Remove the roast and set aside. Add the water or stock to the pot, taking care to scrape up any browned bits from the bottom of the pot. Return the roast to the pot. Press START/STOP to turn off the SEAR/SAUTÉ function. 5. Close the lid and move slider to PRESSURE. Ensuring the pressure release valve is in the SEAL position. The temperature will default to HIGH, which is the correct setting. Set time to 50 minutes. Select START/STOP to begin cooking. 6. When the time is up, quick release the pressure and carefully remove the lid. Shred the meat with two forks and stir in with the liquid in the pot. 7. Divide the meat mixture among the rolls and top each with a slice of pineapple.
Per Serving: Calories 704; Fat 45.87g; Sodium 573mg; Carbs 4.6g; Fibre 0.5g; Sugar 1.2g; Protein 63.96g

Beef Lettuce Wraps

Prep time: 10 minutes | **Cook time:** 20 minutes | **Serves:** 4

2 tbsp olive or avocado oil	1 tsp ground ginger
900 g top sirloin steak or stew meat	2 tbsp cornflour
120 ml soy sauce, gluten-free tamari or coconut aminos	2 tbsp water
60 ml beef stock	1 head romaine lettuce
2 tbsp rice vinegar	120 g matchstick-sliced carrot
3 tbsp coconut sugar	40 g diced green onion
2 tbsp sriracha or chili garlic sauce	10 g chopped fresh coriander (optional)
2 tsp sesame oil	

1. Move slider to AIR FRY/STOVETOP. Select SEAR/SAUTÉ and set to Lo1. Select START/STOP to begin preheating. Heat the oil on the pot and add the meat and brown on all sides. This should take 3 to 4 minutes. Select START/STOP. 2. Combine the soy sauce, coconut sugar, sriracha, beef stock, vinegar, sesame oil and ginger in a medium bowl. Pour the soy sauce mixture over the beef. 3. Close the lid and move slider to PRESSURE. Ensuring the pressure release valve is in the SEAL position. The temperature will default to HIGH, which is the correct setting. Set time to 10 minutes. Select START/STOP to begin cooking. 4. When cooking is complete, naturally release the pressure for 15 minutes. Then release the pressure quickly by turning the pressure release valve to the VENT position. Move slider to AIR FRY/ STOVETOP to unlock the lid, then carefully open it. 5. In a small bowl, stir together the arrowroot starch and water and pour into the pot. Cook on SEAR/SAUTÉ function and set to 3, Select START/STOP to begin cooking. Let the liquid come to a quick boil, then select START/STOP to end the cooking and let the sauce thicken. 6. Assemble the lettuce wraps by adding the beef, carrot, green onion and coriander (if using).

Per Serving: Calories 682; Fat 41.32g; Sodium 671mg; Carbs 24.12g; Fibre 4.3g; Sugar 14.39g; Protein 51.75g

Lemony Beef Risotto

Prep time: 10 minutes | **Cook time:** 15 minutes | **Serves:** 4

900 g. flank steak, thinly sliced	300 ml chicken stock
1 medium onion, thinly sliced	Juice of ½ lemon
3 cloves garlic, minced	Suggested toppings: tzatziki sauce, lettuce, tomato, sliced onion, crumbled feta cheese
250 g uncooked long-grain white rice, rinsed	

1. Move slider to AIR FRY/STOVETOP. Select SEAR/SAUTÉ and set to 3. Select START/STOP to begin preheating. 2. Add the flank steak, onion and garlic to the preheated pot. Cook for about 5 minutes, or until the meat is browned. Press START/STOP to turn off the SEAR/SAUTÉ function. 3. Add the rice, stock and lemon juice, taking care that the rice is completely submerged in the liquid. 4. Close the lid and move slider to PRESSURE. Ensuring the pressure release valve is in the SEAL position. The temperature will default to HIGH, which is the correct setting. Set time to 9 minutes. Select START/STOP to begin cooking. 5. When the timer sounds, quick release the pressure and carefully remove the lid. Serve in bowls and add your desired toppings.

Per Serving: Calories 554; Fat 12.65g; Sodium 231mg; Carbs 50.25g; Fibre 0.9g; Sugar 1.52g; Protein 54.81g

Coffee-Rubbed Steak and Rice Bowls

Prep time: 10 minutes | **Cook time:** 15 minutes | **Serves:** 4

900 g boneless eye round, cut into ½" (1.3-cm) cubes
3 tbsp ground coffee
1 tbsp smoked paprika
1 tbsp light brown sugar
1 tsp onion powder
1 tsp salt
½ tsp freshly ground black pepper
½ tsp crushed red pepper flakes
400 g uncooked brown rice
600 ml water
60 ml beef stock
Optional toppings: hot sauce, Pico de Gallo, avocado, sour cream, jalapeño peppers, shredded lettuce

1. Mix together the beef, brown sugar, paprika, onion powder, coffee, salt, black pepper and red pepper flakes in a big bowl. Stir to evenly coat all the beef. 2. Place the brown rice and water in a heatproof bowl that can fit the pot of your pressure cooker. 3. Pour the beef stock into the pot, then place the coated beef into the stock in an even layer. 4. Then place the bottom layer of the Deluxe Reversible Rack in the lower position in the pot, slightly pressing it down into the beef. Place the bowl of the rice on the rack. 5. Close the lid and move slider to PRESSURE. Ensuring the pressure release valve is in the SEAL position. The temperature will default to HIGH, which is the correct setting. Set time to 15 minutes. Select START/STOP to begin cooking. 6. When cooking is complete, release the pressure quickly by moving the pressure release valve to the VENT position. Move slider to the right to unlock the lid, then carefully open it. 7. Carefully lift the bowl with rice out of the pot with oven mitt–covered hands. Fluff the rice with a fork. Transfer the rice to individual bowls. 8. Remove the rack. Use a slotted spoon to remove the beef and place it on top of the rice. Add whichever additional toppings you desire.
Per Serving: Calories 743; Fat 12.92g; Sodium 773mg; Carbs 76.87g; Fibre 4.1g; Sugar 3.58g; Protein 75.15g

Korean Beef Rolls

Prep time: 10 minutes | **Cook time:** 40 minutes | **Serves:** 8

80 ml beef stock
120 ml soy sauce
75 g light brown sugar
4 cloves garlic, minced
2 tbsp sesame oil
2 tbsp rice vinegar
2 tbsp grated fresh ginger
2 tbsp Korean chili sauce (gochujang)
1.3 kg chuck roast, cut into bite-sized pieces
8 rolls
Toppings: mayonnaise, sliced jalapeño pepper, cucumber, fresh coriander

1. Add the stock, soy sauce, brown sugar, garlic, sesame oil, vinegar, ginger and chili sauce to a bowl and mix well. Pour the mixture into the pot and add the beef. 2. Close the lid and move slider to PRESSURE. Ensuring the pressure release valve is in the SEAL position. The temperature will default to HIGH, which is the correct setting. Set time to 40 minutes. Select START/STOP to begin cooking. 3. When the timer sounds, quick release the pressure and carefully remove the lid. Divide the beef mixture among the rolls and add toppings as desired.
Per Serving: Calories 403; Fat 14.39g; Sodium 1082mg; Carbs 28.47g; Fibre 1.5g; Sugar 6.98g; Protein 37.49g

Herbed Beef & Cheddar Croissants

Prep time: 10 minutes | **Cook time:** 15 minutes | **Serves:** 4-6

- 240 ml beef stock
- 1 (1 – 1.3 kg) eye round roast
- 3 cloves garlic, cut in half
- 1 tbsp extra-virgin olive oil
- 1 tbsp salt
- ¾ tsp freshly ground black pepper, divided
- 1 tsp chopped fresh basil
- 1 tsp chopped fresh rosemary
- 1 tsp chopped fresh parsley
- 2 tbsp unsalted butter
- 2 tbsp flour
- 240 ml milk
- 1 tsp prepared grated horseradish
- ½ tsp paprika
- 1 tsp salt
- 200 g shredded sharp cheddar cheese
- 10 croissants, cut in half

1. Pour the stock into the pot and place the bottom layer of the Deluxe Reversible Rack in the lower position in the pot. 2. Make six 1 cm -deep slits in the surface of the beef round, three on the top and three on the bottom. Insert ½ garlic clove into each slit. 3. Rub the olive oil all over the beef round. Season with the salt , ½ teaspoon of the pepper, rosemary, basil and parsley and rub them all over the surface of the beef. Place the seasoned beef on the rack. 4. Close the lid and move slider to PRESSURE. Ensuring the pressure release valve is in the SEAL position. The temperature will default to HIGH, which is the correct setting. Set time to 3 minutes. Select START/STOP to begin cooking. 5. When the timer beeps, let the pressure naturally release for 2 hours. The pot will switch to keep warm. After 2 hours of the eye round sitting in the pot, it will be rare in the centre . For a well-done beef, let the eye round stay in the pot for 3 hours. 6. While the beef is cooking and resting, you can prepare the cheese sauce by heating butter in a small saucepan over medium heat until melted. 7. Then, whisk in the flour and lower the heat to medium-low. Gradually add milk while whisking, and stir in horseradish, paprika, salt, and ¼ teaspoon of pepper. Cook for 2 to 3 minutes until the milk starts to thicken, and then add the cheese. 8. Stir the cheese into the liquid over low heat until melted, and then remove the pan from the heat. Cover with a lid and let it sit until the beef is done cooking. 9. Once the beef has reached your preferred doneness, remove it with tongs and transfer to a large cutting board. Let the beef rest for 7 to 10 minutes, then thinly slice. 10. Place the sliced beef inside the croissants, topped with a spoonful or two of cheese sauce.

Per Serving: Calories 765; Fat 44.41g; Sodium 1395mg; Carbs 46.64g; Fibre 2.6g; Sugar 12.54g; Protein 43.42g

Easy Beef and Broccoli

Prep time: 15 minutes | **Cook time:** 20 minutes | **Serves:** 2

- 2 teaspoons sesame oil
- 300 g thinly sliced uncooked beef roast
- Freshly ground black pepper
- ½ small onion, chopped
- 3 garlic cloves, minced
- 120 ml Beef Stock
- 60 ml low-sodium soy sauce
- 2 tablespoons packed brown sugar
- Pinch red pepper flakes (optional)
- 1 tablespoon cornflour
- 200 g fresh broccoli florets

1. Move slider to AIR FRY/STOVETOP. Select SEAR/SAUTÉ and set to 3. Select START/STOP to begin preheating. 2. Add the sesame oil to the preheated pot. Season the beef with black pepper, add to the pot, and brown on all sides, about 1 minute per side. Transfer to a plate and set aside. Add the onion and garlic to the pot and sauté until softened, 2 minutes. 3. Add the stock and deglaze the pot, scraping up the browned bits from the bottom with a wooden spoon and stirring them into the liquid. 4. Stir in the soy sauce, brown sugar, and red pepper flakes (if using). Stir until the sugar is dissolved, then return the beef to the pot with any juices from the plate. Press START/STOP to turn off the SEAR/SAUTÉ function. 5. Close the lid and move slider to Pressure. Ensuring the pressure release valve is in the SEAL position. The temperature will default to HIGH, which is the correct setting. Set time to 10 minutes. Select START/STOP to begin cooking. 6. When cooking is complete, release the pressure quickly by turning the pressure release valve to the VENT position. Move slider to the right to unlock the lid, then carefully open it. 7. Cook on SEAR/SAUTÉ function again and set to Hi 5. Transfer about 2 tablespoons of liquid from the pot to a small bowl. 8. Whisk it together with the cornflour, then add back to the pot along with the broccoli. Press START/STOP to begin cooking. 9. Loosely cover with the lid and let simmer for 3 to 4 minutes, or until the sauce is thick and the broccoli is softened. Taste and adjust the seasonings as desired. 10. Serve the beef and broccoli over a scoop of rice and sprinkle with sesame seeds.

Per Serving: Calories 472; Fat 19.69g; Sodium 1444mg; Carbs 22.78g; Fibre 4.1g; Sugar 10.68g; Protein 53.96g

Pulled Beef with Pappardelle

Prep time: 10 minutes | **Cook time:** 55 minutes | **Serves:** 2

2 tablespoons oil, plus more if needed
225 g beef chuck roast, cut into 4 equal pieces
Salt
Freshly ground black pepper
1 small onion, diced
1 carrot, diced
1 celery stalk, diced
3 garlic cloves, smashed
120 ml dry red wine
1 can diced tomatoes with their juices
1 tablespoon tomato paste
120 ml Beef Stock
2 thyme sprigs or ¼ teaspoon dried thyme
1 rosemary sprig, chopped, or ½ teaspoon dried rosemary
1 bay leaf
150 g pappardelle, boiled until al dente

1. Move slider to AIR FRY/STOVETOP. Select SEAR/SAUTÉ and set to Lo1. Select START/STOP to begin preheating. Then add 2 tablespoons of oil and heat until shimmering. Season the beef with salt and pepper, add the beef to the pot and sear for 3 minutes, turning to brown on all sides. Transfer the beef to a plate and set aside. 2. Heat more oil in the pot, if needed, add the onion, carrot, and celery, and cook for 4 to 5 minutes, stirring often, until the vegetables begin to soften. 3. Add the garlic and cook for 1 minute. Stir in the wine and deglaze the pot, scraping up the browned bits from the bottom with a wooden spoon and stirring them into the liquid. Cook until the wine is reduced by half, about 2 minutes, then press START/STOP. 4. Return the beef to the pot and stir in the tomatoes with their juices, the tomato paste, thyme, rosemary, beef stock, and bay leaf and season with salt and pepper. 5. Close the lid and move slider to PRESSURE. Ensuring the pressure release valve is in the SEAL position. The temperature will default to HIGH, which is the correct setting. Set time to 30 minutes. Select START/STOP to begin cooking. 6. When cooking is complete, release the pressure quickly by turning the pressure release valve to the VENT position. Move slider to the right to unlock the lid, then carefully open it. 7. Cook on SEAR/SAUTÉ function again and set to 3. Select START/STOP to begin cooking. 8. Using two forks, shred the beef in the pot. Let the sauce cook down for 10 to 15 minutes, stirring occasionally, until thickened. In the last 3 to 5 minutes, stir in the al dente pasta. Discard the bay leaf. 9. Divide the meat and pasta between two bowls. Top with grated Parmesan cheese and chopped parsley.

Per Serving: Calories 488; Fat 24.34g; Sodium 1052mg; Carbs 32.25g; Fibre 6.1g; Sugar 12.55g; Protein 37.13g

Red Wine-Braised Beef Short Ribs

Prep time: 20 minutes | **Cook time:** 60 minutes | **Serves:** 2

2 tablespoons oil, divided
455 g boneless beef short ribs
Salt
Freshly ground black pepper
½ onion, chopped
1 whole carrot, peeled and chopped
1 celery stalk, chopped
2 garlic cloves, minced
240 ml dry red wine, divided
240 ml Beef Stock
1 rosemary sprig
60 ml water
2 tablespoons cornflour

1. Move slider to AIR FRY/STOVETOP. Select SEAR/SAUTÉ and set to Lo1. Select START/STOP to begin preheating. 2. Add 1 tablespoon of oil to the preheated pot. Season the short ribs with salt and pepper, place them in a single layer in the pot, and sear on both sides for 6 to 7 minutes. 3. Move the ribs onto a plate and leave them there. Put the pot on the heat and pour in one tablespoon of oil. 4. Add onion, carrot, celery, and garlic and cook for approximately 5 minutes until they become soft. Sprinkle salt and pepper to taste. 5. Pour in 120 ml of wine into the pot to deglaze it, and use a wooden spoon to scrape off the browned bits from the bottom of the pot and mix them into the liquid for about 2 to 3 minutes. Press START/STOP to turn off the SEAR/SAUTÉ function. Return the short ribs to the pot. 6. Add the remaining 120 ml of wine, the stock, and the rosemary. Close the lid and move slider to PRESSURE. Ensuring the pressure release valve is in the SEAL position. The temperature will default to HIGH, which is the correct setting. Set time to 35 minutes. Select START/STOP to begin cooking. 7. When cooking is complete, release the pressure quickly by turning the pressure release valve to the VENT position. Move slider to the right to unlock the lid, then carefully open it. Press START/STOP. 8. Transfer the meat to a cutting board and let rest. Using a large, shallow spoon, skim any fat from the surface of the liquid in the pot. 9. Combine the water and cornflour in a small bowl. Cook on SEAR/SAUTÉ function and set to 3. Press START/STOP to begin cooking, 2 to 3 minutes. 10. Whisk in the cornflour mixture and let the liquid boil until it thickens, 4 to 5 minutes. Add the ribs back to the pot and reheat in the gravy. 11. Serve the short ribs and gravy over mashed potatoes, pasta, or polenta.

Per Serving: Calories 585; Fat 34.29g; Sodium 722mg; Carbs 16.13g; Fibre 1.8g; Sugar 3.41g; Protein 49g

Garlicky Pork Roast with Red Cabbage

Prep time: 10 minutes | **Cook time:** 2 hours | **Serves:** 2

2 uncooked bacon slices
345 g boneless pork shoulder roast
2 garlic cloves, peeled and halved
1½ teaspoons red Hawaiian sea salt
240 ml water
½ red cabbage, cored and cut into thirds

1. Move slider to AIR FRY/STOVETOP. Select SEAR/SAUTÉ and set to Lo1. Select START/STOP to begin preheating. Add the bacon to the preheated pot and cook until both sides are browned but not crispy, about 5 minutes. 2. Meanwhile, prepare the pork. Place the roast on a cutting board and use a sharp knife to make four slits in it. Tuck half of a garlic clove into each slit. Rub the sea salt evenly over the meat. 3. Move the bacon to the side of the pot, add the pork, and sear it on both sides in the bacon grease, about 3 minutes per side. 4. Add the water and deglaze the pot, scraping up any browned bits from the bottom with a wooden spoon and making sure the bacon and pork do not stick to the pot. Press START/STOP to turn off the SEAR/SAUTÉ function. 5. Close the lid and move slider to PRESSURE. Ensuring the pressure release valve is in the SEAL position. The temperature will default to HIGH, which is the correct setting. Set time to 90 minutes. Select START/STOP to begin cooking. 6. When cooking is complete, naturally release the pressure for 15 minutes. Then release the pressure quickly by turning the pressure release valve to the VENT position. Move slider to AIR FRY/ STOVETOP to unlock the lid, then carefully open it. 7. Transfer the pork to a large bowl and let rest for 5 minutes. Taste the cooking liquid and add more water or season with more salt if desired. Reserve 60 ml of the cooking liquid and set aside. 8. Add the cabbage to the pot. Secure the lid and cook on high pressure for 4 minutes. Quick release the pressure in the pot, then remove the lid. 9. While the cabbage is cooking, use two forks to shred the pork, adding the reserved liquid to keep it moistened. 10. Serve the pork over rice, with the cabbage on the side.

Per Serving: Calories 400; Fat 17.47g; Sodium 1309mg; Carbs 16.67g; Fibre 4.5g; Sugar 8.28g; Protein 44.53g

Beer–Braised Pork with Sauerkraut

Prep time: 10 minutes | **Cook time:** 30 minutes | **Serves:** 2

2 tablespoons butter or oil
225 g pork (such as roast or loin), cut into 2.5 cm chunks
Salt
Freshly ground black pepper
60 ml beer or stock
½ onion, thinly sliced
400 g jarred sauerkraut with its juices
½ apple, sliced (optional)
115 g fully cooked kielbasa sausage, sliced into 1 cm rounds (optional)

1. Move slider to AIR FRY/STOVETOP. Select SEAR/SAUTÉ and set to 3. Select START/STOP to begin preheating. Once the pot is hot, add the butter to melt. Season the pork with salt and pepper, add to the pot, and sear for 3 minutes, browning the chunks on all sides. 2. Stir in the beer and deglaze the pot, scraping up any browned bits from the bottom with a wooden spoon and stirring them into the liquid. Add the onion and sauté, stirring often, for 2 to 3 minutes, or until the liquid is reduced by half. Press START/STOP to turn off the SEAR/SAUTÉ function. 3. Layer the sauerkraut and its juices and the apple (if using) on top of the pork and onion. 4. Close the lid and move slider to PRESSURE. Ensuring the pressure release valve is in the SEAL position. The temperature will default to HIGH, which is the correct setting. Set time to 15 minutes. Select START/STOP to begin cooking. 5. When cooking is complete, naturally release the pressure for 10 minutes. Then release the pressure quickly by turning the pressure release valve to the VENT position. Move slider to AIR FRY/ STOVETOP to unlock the lid, then carefully open it. 6. Add the kielbasa (if using) and stir the contents of the pot. Close the lid and let the kielbasa warm up in the mixture for 5 to 10 minutes. 7. Serve over a bed of warm mashed potatoes.

Per Serving: Calories 770; Fat 40.28g; Sodium 1018mg; Carbs 11.54g; Fibre 1.2g; Sugar 7.16g; Protein 88.67g

Pulled Lamb Shoulder with Pomegranate & Honey Sauce

Prep time: 10 minutes | **Cook time:** 1½ hours | **Serves:** 8

480 ml pomegranate juice
1 medium lemon, scrubbed to remove any waxy coating, then quartered, seeded, and finely chopped
4 medium garlic cloves, peeled and minced (4 teaspoons)
1 tablespoon dried oregano
2 teaspoons ground cinnamon
2 teaspoons dried dill
1 teaspoon table salt
One 1.3 kg bone-in lamb shoulder
1 large red onion, thinly sliced and broken into rings
2 tablespoons honey

1. Pour the pomegranate juice into the pot. In a small mixing bowl, combine the lemon, cinnamon, dill, garlic, oregano, and salt. Pat and rub this mixture evenly over the lamb shoulder. Set the meat in the cooker, scatter the onions all around and on the meat. Close the lid and move slider to PRESSURE. 2. Ensuring the pressure release valve is in the SEAL position. The temperature will default to HIGH, which is the correct setting. Set time to 1 hour 10 minutes. Select START/STOP to begin cooking. 3. When cooking is complete, naturally release the pressure for 30 minutes. Then release the pressure quickly by turning the pressure release valve to the VENT position. Move slider to AIR FRY/ STOVETOP to unlock the lid, then carefully open it. 4. Use a meat fork and a large, slotted spoon to transfer the meat (whole or in pieces) to a cutting board. 5. Shred the meat with two forks, discarding the bone as well as any additional bits of cartilage or fat. Then use a flatware tablespoon to skim any excess surface fat from the sauce in the pot. 6. Move slider to AIR FRY/STOVETOP. Select SEAR/SAUTÉ and set to 3. Select START/STOP to begin cooking. 7. Bring the sauce to a simmer, stirring occasionally. Stir in the honey and cook, stirring more and more frequently, until reduced to about half its volume, 5 to 10 minutes. 8. Stir the meat into the sauce and cook, stirring to coat every thread of meat, for 1 minute. Press START/STOP to turn off the SEAR/SAUTÉ function. 9. Close the lid and set aside for 5 to 10 minutes to blend the flavours and allow the meat to continue to absorb the sauce.

Per Serving: Calories 532; Fat 34.01g; Sodium 958mg; Carbs 16.44g; Fibre 1.2g; Sugar 13.19g; Protein 38.57g

Pork Chops with Creamy Mushroom Gravy

Prep time: 10 minutes | **Cook time:** 35 minutes | **Serves:** 2

1 tablespoon oil
2 bone-in, medium-cut pork chops
Salt
Freshly ground black pepper
½ small onion, sliced
100 g cremini mushrooms, sliced
2 garlic cloves, minced
Splash of dry white wine
240 ml chicken stock
1 tablespoon cornflour
180 g sour cream
1 tablespoon butter

1. Move slider to AIR FRY/STOVETOP. Select SEAR/SAUTÉ and set to Lo1. Select START/STOP to begin preheating. Allow unit to preheat for 5 minutes, add the oil. 2. Season the pork chops generously with salt and pepper, sear on both sides, and transfer to a plate. 3. Then, add the onion, mushrooms, and garlic and sauté until softened, 3 minutes. Pour in the white wine and deglaze the pot, scraping up any browned bits from the bottom with a wooden spoon and stirring them into the liquid. 4. Add the stock and stir. Set the seared pork chops in the pot. Press START/STOP. Close the lid and move slider to PRESSURE. 5. Ensuring the pressure release valve is in the SEAL position. The temperature will default to HIGH, which is the correct setting. Set time to 8 minutes. Select START/STOP to begin cooking. 6. When cooking is complete, naturally release the pressure for 10 minutes. Then release the pressure quickly by turning the pressure release valve to the VENT position. Move slider to AIR FRY/STOVETOP to unlock the lid, then carefully open it. Press START/STOP. 7. Transfer the pork chops to a plate. Cook on SEAR/SAUTÉ function again and set to 3. Press START/STOP to begin cooking. 8. Remove 1 tablespoon of cooking liquid from the pot and put in a small bowl with the cornflour . 9. Whisk well, then return the mixture to the pot and whisk in the sour cream and butter until combined. Simmer to thicken, 4 to 5 minutes. Season with more salt and pepper if desired. 10. Serve with mashed potatoes and steamed vegetables, and garnish with parsley.
Per Serving: Calories 795; Fat 41.11g; Sodium 617mg; Carbs 59.62g; Fibre 7g; Sugar 4.2g; Protein 52.2g

Barbecue Beef & Pasta Casserole

Prep time: 10 minutes | **Cook time:** 15 minutes | **Serves:** 4

2 tablespoons vegetable, corn, or rapeseed oil
1 large yellow onion, chopped
1 medium green pepper , stemmed, cored, and sliced into thin strips
600 g lean beef mince
48 ml beef or chicken stock
300 g barbecue sauce
200 g dried rigatoni

1. Move slider to AIR FRY/STOVETOP. Select SEAR/SAUTÉ and set to 3. Select START/STOP to begin preheating. Add the oil to the pot and heat for 1-2 minutes. 2. Add the onion and pepper ; cook, stirring frequently, until the onion begins to soften, about 4 minutes. 3. Crumble in the beef mince and cook, stirring often to break up any clumps, until lightly browned, about 4 minutes. 4. Pour in the stock and scrape up every speck of browned stuff on the pot's bottom. Press START/STOP to turn off the SEAR/SAUTÉ function. 5. Stir in the barbecue sauce and pasta. Close the lid and move slider to PRESSURE. Ensuring the pressure release valve is in the SEAL position. The temperature will default to HIGH, which is the correct setting. Set time to 5 minutes. Select START/STOP to begin cooking. 6. When cooking is complete, release the pressure quickly by turning the pressure release valve to the VENT position. Move slider to the right to unlock the lid, then carefully open it. Stir well before serving.
Per Serving: Calories 791; Fat 35.89g; Sodium 1175mg; Carbs 45g; Fibre 2g; Sugar 32.68g; Protein 68.4g

Beef, Barley and Celery Soup

Prep time: 10 minutes | **Cook time:** 50 minutes | **Serves:** 6

1 tablespoon vegetable, corn, or rapeseed oil
3 bone-in beef short ribs (about 675 g)
120 g frozen pearl onions (do not thaw)
2 medium celery ribs, thinly sliced
6 medium garlic cloves, peeled and minced (2 tablespoons)
1.4 L beef or chicken stock
185 g pearl barley
1 tablespoon stemmed fresh thyme leaves
½ teaspoon ground allspice
½ teaspoon table salt
½ teaspoon ground black pepper
1 tablespoon balsamic vinegar

1. Move slider to AIR FRY/STOVETOP. Select SEAR/SAUTÉ and set to 3. Select START/STOP to begin preheating. 2. Add oil to the preheated pot and heat for 1-2 minutes. Add the short ribs and brown well on all sides, turning several times, about 10 minutes. 3. Transfer the short ribs to a bowl. Add the pearl onions and celery to the pot. 4. Cook, stirring frequently, until the onions begin to brown a bit, about 4 minutes. 5. Stir in the garlic until fragrant, just a few seconds. Pour in the stock, press START/STOP to turn off the SEAR/SAUTÉ function. Scrape up every single browned speck on the pot's bottom. 6. Stir in the barley, allspice, thyme, salt, and pepper. Return the short ribs to the pot, as well as any liquid in their bowl. 7. Close the lid and move slider to PRESSURE. Ensuring the pressure release valve is in the SEAL position. The temperature will default to HIGH, which is the correct setting. Set time to 35 minutes. Select START/STOP to begin cooking. 8. When cooking is complete, naturally release the pressure for 40 minutes. Then release the pressure quickly by turning the pressure release valve to the VENT position. Move slider to AIR FRY/ STOVETOP to unlock the lid, then carefully open it. 9. Transfer the short ribs to a large cutting board; cool for 5 minutes. 10. In the meantime, use a flatware tablespoon to skim any excess surface fat from the soup in the pot. Remove and discard the bones; chop the meat into small bits. 11. Stir the meat as well as the balsamic vinegar into the soup, then serve warm.
Per Serving: Calories 371; Fat 15.36g; Sodium 1176mg; Carbs 32.03g; Fibre 6.1g; Sugar 3.09g; Protein 27.44g

Tasty Pickled Pulled Pork

Prep time: 10 minutes | **Cook time:** 1 hour | **Serves:** 8

360 ml jarred pickle brine
1 teaspoon dried dill
1 teaspoon ground coriander
1 teaspoon ground dried mustard
1 teaspoon table salt
½ teaspoon red pepper flakes
1.3 kg boneless pork shoulder, cut in half and any large chunks of fat removed

1. Pour the brine into the pot of your Ninja XL Pressure Cooker. 2. In a small bowl, combine the dill, dried mustard, coriander, salt, and pepper flakes. Spread this mixture evenly over the pork. Set the pork in the pot. 3. Close the lid and move slider to PRESSURE. Ensuring the pressure release valve is in the SEAL position. The temperature will default to HIGH, which is the correct setting. Set time to 60 minutes. Select START/STOP to begin cooking. 4. When cooking is complete, naturally release the pressure for 30 minutes. Then release the pressure quickly by turning the pressure release valve to the VENT position. Move slider to AIR FRY/ STOVETOP to unlock the lid, then carefully open it. 5. To move the pork to a cutting board, use a meat fork and a slotted spoon. Remove any extra fat from the sauce using a flatware tablespoon. 6. Shred the meat with two forks and put it back into the pot with the flavourful liquid. 7. While there may be excess liquid, leave the shredded meat in it to absorb more flavour. Use tongs to take out individual servings.
Per Serving: Calories 222; Fat 6g; Sodium 600mg; Carbs 1.13g; Fibre 0.4g; Sugar 0.45g; Protein 38.64g

Beer-Braised Pulled Beef

Prep time: 10 minutes | **Cook time:** 75 minutes | **Serves:** 6

1 tablespoon vegetable, corn, or rapeseed oil
One 1.1 kg boneless beef chuck roast, cut into two chunks and any large bits of fat removed
½ teaspoon table salt
½ teaspoon ground black pepper
120 ml amber beer, preferably a pilsner or a pale ale (a gluten-free beer, if necessary)
180 ml beef stock
80 g jarred prepared white horseradish
2 tablespoons Worcestershire sauce
1 teaspoon dried ground ginger
½ teaspoon ground dried turmeric
2 medium garlic cloves, peeled and minced
2 bay leaves

1. Move slider to AIR FRY/STOVETOP. Select SEAR/SAUTÉ and set to 3. Select START/STOP to begin preheating. Add oil to the pot and heat for 1-2 minutes. 2. In the meantime, season the beef with the salt and pepper. Add one piece to the pot and brown it well, flipping once or twice, about 7 minutes. 3. Transfer to a bowl and add the second piece of beef. Brown this one just as well on both sides before transferring it to the bowl. Pour the beer into the pot. Scrape up the browned stuff on the pot's bottom. Press START/STOP to turn off the SEAR/SAUTÉ function. 4. Stir in the stock, Worcestershire sauce, horseradish, garlic, ginger, turmeric, and bay leaves. Nestle the pieces of beef into this sauce, turning them to coat them on all sides. 5. Close the lid and move slider to PRESSURE. Ensuring the pressure release valve is in the SEAL position. The temperature will default to HIGH, which is the correct setting. Set time to 55 minutes. Select START/STOP to begin cooking. 6. When cooking is complete, naturally release the pressure for 30 minutes. Then release the pressure quickly by turning the pressure release valve to the VENT position. Move slider to AIR FRY/ STOVETOP to unlock the lid, then carefully open it. 7. Use a meat fork and a large, slotted spoon to transfer the pieces of meat to a nearby cutting board. 8. Use a flatware tablespoon to skim any excess surface fat off the sauce. Also find and discard the garlic cloves and the bay leaves. Cook on SEAR/SAUTÉ function again and set to 3. Select START/STOP to begin cooking. 9. Bring the sauce to a simmer, stirring frequently. Simmer until thickened like a loose, wet barbecue sauce, stirring almost all the while, 5 to 10 minutes. In the meantime, shred the meat with two forks. 10. When the sauce has reached the right consistency, stir the meat into it and cook, stirring often, until well coated and most of the liquid has been absorbed, about 1 minute. 11. Turn off the SEAR/SAUTÉ function and close the lid, let it stand for 5 minutes to blend the flavours and let the meat absorb more sauce. 12. You can serve this pulled beef on potato rolls with horseradish cream sauce.

Per Serving: Calories 405; Fat 18.53g; Sodium 540mg; Carbs 9.23g; Fibre 1g; Sugar 2.48g; Protein 51.19g

Teriyaki Pulled Lamb

Prep time: 10 minutes | **Cook time:** 1 hour 20 minutes | **Serves:** 8

- 1 tablespoon dark brown sugar
- 2 teaspoons mild smoked paprika
- 1½ teaspoons ground cumin
- 1 teaspoon ground dried mustard
- 1 teaspoon onion powder
- 1 teaspoon ground black pepper
- ½ teaspoon garlic powder
- One 1.3 kg boneless leg of lamb, any netting removed, the meat opened up, cut in half, and any large chunks of fat removed
- 240 ml beef stock
- 60 ml apple cider vinegar
- 2 tablespoons soy sauce

1. In a large mixing bowl, combine the brown sugar, cumin, dried mustard, smoked paprika, black pepper, onion powder, and garlic powder. Pat the spice mixture over all sides of the lamb. 2. Add the stock, vinegar, and soy sauce to the pot. Set the meat into this sauce (do not turn over to coat). 3. Close the lid and move slider to PRESSURE. Ensuring the pressure release valve is in the SEAL position. The temperature will default to HIGH, which is the correct setting. Set time to 1 hour 5 minutes. Select START/STOP to begin cooking. 4. When cooking is complete, naturally release the pressure for 30 minutes. Then release the pressure quickly by turning the pressure release valve to the VENT position. Move slider to AIR FRY/ STOVETOP to unlock the lid, then carefully open it. 5. Use a meat fork and a big, slotted spoon to transfer the meat (whole or in pieces) to a cutting board. Shred the meat with two forks. Then use a flatware tablespoon to skim any excess surface fat from the sauce. 6. Move slider to AIR FRY/STOVETOP. Select SEAR/SAUTÉ and set to 3. Select START/STOP to begin cooking. 7. Heat the sauce on high heat until it reaches a full simmer, stirring occasionally. Continue cooking and stirring the sauce until it reduces to half its original volume, which should take around 5 to 8 minutes. 8. Then, mix the shredded meat into the sauce and stir well to ensure that the meat is fully coated. 9. Cook this mixture for another minute while stirring constantly. 10. Once done, turn off the SEAR/SAUTÉ function and let the dish sit for 5 to 10 minutes before serving.

Per Serving: Calories 276; Fat 11.83g; Sodium 275mg; Carbs 4.76g; Fibre 0.7g; Sugar 3.03g; Protein 35.8g

Chapter 7 Dessert Recipes

Vanilla Cheesecake

Prep time: 20 minutes | **Cook time:** 65 minutes | **Serves:** 6

240 g water
40 g digestive biscuit crumbs
1 tbsp. plus 140 g sugar, divided
¼ tsp. ground cinnamon
Topping (optional):
100 g. white baking chocolate, chopped
3 tbsp. heavy whipping cream

2½ tbsp. butter, melted
2 pkg. (200 g each) cream cheese, softened
2 to 3 tsp. vanilla extract
2 large eggs, lightly beaten

Sliced fresh strawberries or raspberries, optional

1. Grease a 15 cm springform pan; pour water into the pot of your Ninja XL Pressure Cooker. Mix cracker crumbs, 1 tbsp. sugar and cinnamon; stir in butter. Press onto bottom and about 2.5 cmup sides of the prepared pan. 2. In a separate bowl, beat cream cheese and remaining sugar until smooth. Beat in vanilla. Add the eggs and beat on low speed just until combined. Pour over crust. 3. Cover cheesecake tightly with foil. Then place the bottom layer of the Deluxe Reversible Rack in the lower position in the pot. Place springform pan on the rack in the pot. 4. Close the lid and move slider to PRESSURE. Ensuring the pressure release valve is in the SEAL position. The temperature will default to LOW, which is the correct setting. Set time to 1 hour and 5 minutes. Select START/STOP to begin cooking. 5. When cooking is complete, release the pressure quickly by moving the pressure release valve to the VENT position. Move slider to the right to unlock the lid, then carefully open it. 6. Carefully remove springform pan from pressure cooker; remove foil. Cool cheesecake on a wire rack for 1 hour. 7. To release the cheesecake from the pan, use a knife to loosen the sides. 8. Then, refrigerate the cheesecake overnight and cover it once it has completely cooled. 9. To make the topping, melt chocolate and cream in a microwave, stir until it becomes smooth, and let it cool for a bit. Remove the rim from the springform pan and pour the chocolate mixture over the cheesecake. You can sprinkle berries on top if you wish to serve.

Per Serving: Calories 374; Fat 29.38g; Sodium 399mg; Carbs 21.37g; Fibre 0.1g; Sugar 19.78g; Protein 6.76g

Homemade Molten Mocha Cake

Prep time: 10 minutes | **Cook time:** 25 minutes | **Serves:** 6

240 ml water
4 large eggs
300 g sugar
115 g butter, melted
1 tbsp. vanilla extract
125 g plain flour

50 g baking cocoa
1 tbsp. instant coffee granules
¼ tsp. Salt
Fresh raspberries or sliced fresh strawberries and vanilla ice cream, optional

1. Pour water into the pot. Mix together the eggs, butter, sugar and vanilla in a large bowl and toss well. In a separate bowl, whisk flour, coffee granules, cocoa and salt; gradually beat into egg mixture. 2. Transfer the mixture to a greased baking dish that can fit the pot. Cover loosely with foil to prevent moisture from getting into dish. 3. Then place the bottom layer of the Deluxe Reversible Rack in the lower position in the pot. 4. Place the pan on the rack. Close the lid and move slider to PRESSURE. Ensuring the pressure release valve is in the SEAL position. The temperature will default to HIGH, which is the correct setting. Set time to 25 minutes. Select START/STOP to begin cooking. 5. When cooking is complete, naturally release the pressure for 10 minutes. Then release the pressure quickly by turning the pressure release valve to the VENT position. Move slider to AIR FRY/ STOVETOP to unlock the lid, then carefully open it. 6. A toothpick should come out with moist crumbs. If desired, serve warm cake with berries and ice cream.
Per Serving: Calories 373; Fat 19.5g; Sodium 228mg; Carbs 47.19g; Fibre 2.9g; Sugar 25.93g; Protein 5.51g

Cheesecake with Peaches

Prep time: 25 minutes | **Cook time:** 30 minutes | **Serves:** 6

1 pkg. (200 g) reduced-fat cream cheese
100 g fat-free cream cheese
100 g sugar
120 g reduced-fat sour cream
2 tbsp. unsweetened apple juice

1 tbsp. flour
½ tsp. vanilla
3 large eggs, room temperature, lightly beaten
2 medium ripe peaches, peeled and thinly sliced

1. Add 240 ml water to the pot and place the bottom layer of the Deluxe Reversible Rack in the lower position in the pot. 2. Grease a 15 cm springform pan; place on a double thickness of heavy-duty foil. Wrap securely around pan. 3. In a bowl, beat cream cheeses and sugar until smooth. 4. Beat in flour, sour cream, apple juice, and vanilla. Add the eggs; beat on low speed just until blended. Pour into the prepared pan. 5. Cover pan with foil. Fold an 46x30 cmpiece of foil lengthwise into thirds, making a sling. Use the sling to lower the pan on the rack in the pot of your pressure cooker. 6. Close the lid and move slider to PRESSURE. Ensuring the pressure release valve is in the SEAL position. The temperature will default to HIGH, which is the correct setting. Set time to 30 minutes. Select START/STOP to begin cooking. 7. When cooking is complete, naturally release the pressure for 10 minutes. Then release the pressure quickly by turning the pressure release valve to the VENT position. Move slider to AIR FRY/ STOVETOP to unlock the lid, then carefully open it. 8. Using foil sling, carefully remove the springform pan. Let it sit for 10 minutes. Remove foil from the pan. Cool the cheesecake on a wire rack for about 1 hour. 9. Loosen sides from pan with a knife. Refrigerate overnight, covering when cooled. To serve, remove rim from springform pan. Serve with peaches.
Per Serving: Calories 202; Fat 8.7g; Sodium 308mg; Carbs 22.7g; Fibre 0.8g; Sugar 16.38g; Protein 8.64g

Classic Cheesecake

Prep time: 15 minutes | **Cook time:** 35 minutes | **Serves:** 8

Nonstick cooking spray
16 crushed digestive biscuits
4 tablespoons unsalted butter, melted
2 tablespoons granulated sugar
400 g cream cheese, at room temperature
110 g brown sugar
60 g sour cream
1 tablespoon flour
½ teaspoon fine sea salt
2 teaspoons vanilla extract
2 large eggs, at room temperature
480 ml water, for steaming

1. Line the bottom of a 18 cm springform pan with a piece of parchment paper and grease with nonstick cooking spray. 2. Mix together the butter, graham cracker crumbs, and granulated sugar in a large bowl and mix until moist. Pour the mixture into the prepared pan and press firmly to the bottom and up the sides about 5 cm. 3. In another mixing bowl, use an electric mixer to beat the cream cheese and brown sugar until creamy. Add the sour cream and mix, scraping the sides of the bowl. Add the flour, salt, and vanilla and stir to combine. Add the eggs, one at a time, and stir just until incorporated; do not overbeat. 4. Pour the mixture into the prepared crust. Cover the pan with a paper towel and then aluminum foil. 5. Pour the water into the pot and place the bottom layer of the Deluxe Reversible Rack in the lower position in the pot. Place the pan on the rack. 6. Close the lid and move slider to PRESSURE. Ensuring the pressure release valve is in the SEAL position. The temperature will default to HIGH, which is the correct setting. Set time to 35 minutes. Select START/STOP to begin cooking. 7. When cooking is complete, naturally release the pressure for 20 minutes. Then release the pressure quickly by turning the pressure release valve to the VENT position. Move slider to AIR FRY/ STOVETOP to unlock the lid, then carefully open it. 8. Using the sling, lift the pan out of the pot. Allow the cheesecake to cool on a cooling rack to room temperature and then refrigerated, still covered with foil, for at least 4 hours before serving.
Per Serving: Calories 303; Fat 22.25g; Sodium 419mg; Carbs 20.84g; Fibre 0.1g; Sugar 18.04g; Protein 5.46g

Delicious Stuffed Peaches

Prep time: 10 minutes | **Cook time:** 3 minutes | **Serves:** 6

2 tbsp butter
⅛ tsp sea salt
50 g sugar
30 g flour
50 g tsp pure almond extract
½ tsp ground cinnamon
5-6 medium peaches, cored
240 ml water

1. Mix together the flour, butter, salt, almond extract, sugar, and cinnamon in a bowl. Stuff each peach with the mixture. 2. Pour water into the pot and place bottom layer of the Deluxe Reversible Rack in the lower position in the pot. 3. Carefully put the peaches on the rack. 4. Add the leftover filling to the pot. Close the lid and move slider to PRESSURE. Ensuring the pressure release valve is in the SEAL position. The temperature will default to HIGH, which is the correct setting. Set time to 3 minutes. Select START/STOP to begin cooking. 5. When cooking is complete, release the pressure quickly by turning the pressure release valve to the VENT position. Move slider to the right to unlock the lid, then carefully open it. 6. Allow to cool for 10-12 minutes. Serve.
Per Serving: Calories 199; Fat 8.96g; Sodium 83mg; Carbs 28.74g; Fibre 3.5g; Sugar 21.21g; Protein 3.84g

Peach-Berry Cobbler

Prep time: 5 minutes | **Cook time:** 15 minutes | **Serves:** 4

2 cans peach pie filling
120 g fresh berries
3 tablespoons unsalted butter, melted
1 large egg
120 gGreek yogurt (for homemade)

70 g granulated sugar
½ teaspoon vanilla extract
150 g plain flour
2 teaspoons baking powder
240 ml water, for steaming

1. Place the peach pie filling in the bottom of a 16 cm round cake pan. Add the berries and gently fold them in. 2. Combine the butter, sugar, egg, yogurt, and vanilla in a bowl, mix well. 3. In a small bowl, mix together the flour and baking powder, and add to the wet ingredients. Stir until combined. The batter should be fairly stiff. 4. Spoon the topping over the top of the fruit. It's okay if the topping is slightly uneven or doesn't completely cover the fruit. Cover the pan with aluminum foil to prevent water from getting into the cobbler. 5. Add water to the pot and place the bottom layer of the Deluxe Reversible Rack in the lower position in the pot. 6. Place the pan on the rack. Close the lid and move slider to PRESSURE. Ensuring the pressure release valve is in the SEAL position. The temperature will default to HIGH, which is the correct setting. Set time to 15 minutes. Select START/STOP to begin cooking. 7. When cooking is complete, naturally release the pressure for 10 minutes. Then release the pressure quickly by turning the pressure release valve to the VENT position. Move slider to AIR FRY/ STOVETOP to unlock the lid, then carefully open it. 8. Lift the cobbler out of the pot. Remove the foil and allow it to rest for 5 minutes.

Per Serving: Calories 669; Fat g10.76; Sodium 260mg; Carbs 140.56g; Fibre 5.1g; Sugar 62.28g; Protein 7.22g

Chocolate-Berry Mug Cake

Prep time: 10 minutes | **Cook time:** 10 minutes | **Serves:** 2

35 g almond flour
1 egg, beaten
1 tbsp maple syrup
1½ tbsp chocolate chips

60 g berries of choice (blueberries, strawberries, raspberries)
½ tsp vanilla
Salt to taste

1. Add the flour, egg, maple syrup, berries, chocolate chips, vanilla, and salt to a small bowl. Mix well. 2. Pour the mixture in a mug that can fit into the pot. 3. Cover the mug tightly with aluminum foil. Add water to the pot and place the bottom layer of the Deluxe Reversible Rack in the lower position in the pot. 4. Place the mug on the rack. Close the lid and move slider to PRESSURE. Ensuring the pressure release valve is in the SEAL position. The temperature will default to HIGH, which is the correct setting. Set time to 10 minutes. Select START/STOP to begin cooking. 5. When cooking is complete, release the pressure quickly by turning the pressure release valve to the VENT position. Move slider to the right to unlock the lid, then carefully open it. 6. Let the cake cool for a few minutes and serve.

Per Serving: Calories 177; Fat 10.39g; Sodium 172mg; Carbs 13.28g; Fibre 2.6g; Sugar 8.37g; Protein 6.35g

Caramel Brownie Pudding

Prep time: 15 minutes | **Cook time:** 25 minutes | **Serves:** 4

Nonstick cooking spray
115 g unsalted butter
200 g dark chocolate chips
200 g granulated sugar
2 teaspoons vanilla extract
2 large eggs
90 g plain flour
90 g pecans, chopped, divided
1 (300 g) jar caramel sauce, divided
240 ml hot water, for steaming
1 (300 g) jar hot fudge sauce

1. Grease a 16 cm round cake pan with nonstick cooking spray. 2. In a medium bowl, mix the butter and chocolate chips and melt them together in the microwave, stirring occasionally. Add the sugar and vanilla and stir until combined. Mix in the eggs, one at a time, stirring until no streaks of egg remain. Stir in the flour. Fold in 60 g of pecans. 3. Transfer the batter to the prepared pan. Add ¼ of caramel sauce and use a spoon to swirl it into the brownie batter. Cover the pan with aluminum foil. 4. Add water to the pot and place the bottom layer of the Deluxe Reversible Rack in the lower position in the pot. 5. Place the pan on the rack. Close the lid and move slider to PRESSURE. Ensuring the pressure release valve is in the SEAL position. The temperature will default to HIGH, which is the correct setting. Set time to 25 minutes. Select START/STOP to begin cooking. 6. When cooking is complete, release the pressure quickly by turning the pressure release valve to the VENT position. Move slider to the right to unlock the lid, then carefully open it. 7. Using the sling, remove the pan and then remove foil. The centre will look undercooked, but it's okay. 8. The consistency is going to be somewhere between a cake-like brownie and chocolate pudding. Allow it to cool. 9. Drizzle with the remaining caramel sauce and the hot fudge and garnish with the remaining 30 g of pecans.

Per Serving: Calories 880; Fat 55.84g; Sodium 1398mg; Carbs 85.08g; Fibre 12.1g; Sugar 46.82g; Protein 13.81g

Red Wine–Braised Apples

Prep time: 10 minutes | **Cook time:** 10 minutes | **Serves:** 6

6 medium apples, cored
1 tsp cinnamon powder
100 g white sugar
25 g raisins
240 ml red wine

1. Add the apples to the pot. Add the cinnamon, raisins, sugar, and red wine, toss to coat. 2. Close the lid and move slider to PRESSURE. Ensuring the pressure release valve is in the SEAL position. The temperature will default to HIGH, which is the correct setting. Set time to 10 minutes. Select START/STOP to begin cooking. 3. When cooking is complete, naturally release the pressure for 10 minutes. Then release the pressure quickly by turning the pressure release valve to the VENT position. Move slider to AIR FRY/ STOVETOP to unlock the lid, then carefully open it. 4. Transfer the apples to a serving plate. 5. Pour the remaining liquid over the apples and serve.

Per Serving: Calories 149; Fat 3.55g; Sodium 6mg; Carbs 31.75g; Fibre 5.2g; Sugar 23.8g; Protein 1.31g

Best Key Lime Pie

Prep time: 10 minutes | **Cook time:** 30 minutes | **Serves:** 6

Crust:
6 crushed digestive biscuits
3 tablespoons melted butter
Key Lime Filling:
300 g cream cheese, cubed and room temperature
Zest of 4 key limes, grated
2 tablespoons sour cream, room temperature
1 tablespoon fresh key lime juice
100 g sugar
1 teaspoon vanilla extract
2 large eggs, room temperature
480 ml water

1. Grease a 16 cm springform pan and set aside. 2. First, use a food processor to crush digestive biscuits into crumbs. Mix the crumbs with melted butter in the food processor and blend. Put the crumb mixture into a springform pan and press it down onto the bottom and partially up the sides of the pan. 3. Place a square of aluminum foil on the outside bottom of the pan and fold it up around the edges. 4. Next, using the food processor, mix cream cheese, sour cream, and sugar until the mixture becomes smooth. Slowly add in eggs, vanilla, key lime zest, and juice, and pulse for 10 seconds. Scrape the edges of the bowl and continue to pulse until the batter becomes smooth. 5. Transfer the batter into springform pan. Pour the water into the pot of your Ninja XL Pressure Cooker. Then place the bottom layer of the Deluxe Reversible Rack in the lower position in the pot. Place the springform pan on the rack. 6. Close the lid and move slider to PRESSURE. Ensuring the pressure release valve is in the SEAL position. The temperature will default to HIGH, which is the correct setting. Set time to 30 minutes. Select START/STOP to begin cooking. 7. When cooking is complete, release the pressure quickly by turning the pressure release valve to the VENT position. Move slider to the right to unlock the lid, then carefully open it. 8. Lift pan out of the pot. Let it cool at room temperature for 10 minutes. 9. The cheesecake will be a little jiggly in the centre . Refrigerate for a minimum of 2 hours to continue to allow it to set. Release side pan and serve.
Per Serving: Calories 307; Fat 24.84g; Sodium 325mg; Carbs 17.76g; Fibre 1.3g; Sugar 11.33g; Protein 5.66g

Lemony Tapioca Pudding

Prep time: 10 minutes | **Cook time:** 10 minutes | **Serves:** 2-4

360 g milk
50 g sugar
95 g tapioca
Zest of 1 lemon

1. Pour the water into the pot and place the bottom layer of the Deluxe Reversible Rack in the lower position in the pot. 2. In a baking dish that can fit into the pot, combine the milk, tapioca, sugar and lemon zest. 3. Place the baking dish on the rack. Close the lid and move slider to PRESSURE. Ensuring the pressure release valve is in the SEAL position. The temperature will default to HIGH, which is the correct setting. Set time to 10 minutes. Select START/STOP to begin cooking. 4. When cooking is complete, release the pressure quickly by turning the pressure release valve to the VENT position. Move slider to the right to unlock the lid, then carefully open it. Serve.
Per Serving: Calories 201; Fat 4.03g; Sodium mg; Carbs 37.72g; Fibre 0.3g; Sugar 15.56g; Protein 3.95g

Vanilla Lemon Cheesecake

Prep time: 10 minutes | **Cook time:** 30 minutes | **Serves:** 6

Crust:
20 vanilla wafers
1½ tablespoons almond slices, toasted
3 tablespoons melted butter
Cheesecake Filling:
300 g cream cheese, cubed and room temperature
2 tablespoons sour cream, room temperature
100 g sugar
2 large eggs, room temperature
Zest of 2 lemons, grated
1 tablespoon fresh lemon juice
1 teaspoon vanilla extract
480 ml water

1. Prepare a 16 cm springform pan by greasing it, then use a food processor to combine vanilla wafers, almonds, and melted butter. 2. Put the mixture into the springform pan and press it down on the bottom and about a third of the way up the sides. 3. Cover the outside of the bottom of the pan with aluminum foil, crimping it up around the edges. 4. Cream together cream cheese, sour cream, and sugar using a hand blender or food processor until smooth, then slowly add eggs, lemon zest, lemon juice, and vanilla extract. 5. Pulse for another 10 seconds and scrape the bowl until the batter is smooth. Transfer the batter into the springform pan. 6. Pour the water into the pot of your Ninja XL Pressure Cooker. Then place the bottom layer of the Deluxe Reversible Rack in the lower position in the pot. 7. Place the springform pan on the rack. Close the lid and move slider to PRESSURE. Ensuring the pressure release valve is in the SEAL position. The temperature will default to HIGH, which is the correct setting. Set time to 30 minutes. Select START/STOP to begin cooking. 8. When cooking is complete, release the pressure quickly by turning the pressure release valve to the VENT position. Move slider to the right to unlock the lid, then carefully open it. 9. Lift pan out of the pot. Let cool at room temperature for 10 minutes. 10. The cheesecake will be a little jiggly in the centre. Refrigerate for a minimum of 2 hours to allow it to set. Release side pan and serve.
Per Serving: Calories 341; Fat 26.12g; Sodium 353mg; Carbs 22.04g; Fibre 0.3g; Sugar 15.75g; Protein 5.92g

Cranberry & Walnuts Stuffed Apples

Prep time: 10 minutes | **Cook time:** 5 minutes | **Serves:** 6

120 ml water
2 tbsp walnuts, chopped
⅛ tsp ground nutmeg
40 g fresh cranberries, chopped
55 g brown sugar
¼ tsp cinnamon powder
5 medium apples, cored

1. Mix together the walnuts, sugar, nutmeg, cranberries, and cinnamon in a bowl. 2. Stuff each apple with the mixture. 3. Pour the water in the pot and add the apples. 4. Add the leftover filling to the pot. Close the lid and move slider to PRESSURE. 5. Ensuring the pressure release valve is in the SEAL position. The temperature will default to HIGH, which is the correct setting. Set time to 5 minutes. Select START/STOP to begin cooking. 6. When cooking is complete, naturally release the pressure for 10 minutes. Then release the pressure quickly by turning the pressure release valve to the VENT position. Move slider to AIR FRY/ STOVETOP to unlock the lid, then carefully open it. 7. Serve.
Per Serving: Calories 138; Fat 1.83g; Sodium 5mg; Carbs 32.19g; Fibre 3.9g; Sugar 26.34g; Protein 1.04g

Easy White Chocolate Pots De Crème

Prep time: 15 minutes | **Cook time:** 20 minutes | **Serves:** 4

4 large egg yolks
2 tablespoons sugar
Pinch of salt
¼ teaspoon vanilla extract

360 ml milk
80 g white chocolate chips
480 ml water

1. First, mix egg yolks, sugar, salt, and vanilla in a small bowl and keep it aside. Then, heat milk in a saucepan over medium-low heat until it reaches a low simmer. 2. Next, take a spoonful of the hot mixture and whisk it into the egg mixture to temper the eggs. Slowly pour this egg mixture into the saucepan with the remaining milk. 3. Add white chocolate chips and stir continuously over a simmer until the chocolate melts, which takes around 10 minutes. 4. Once the chocolate is melted, remove the mixture from heat and distribute it evenly among four custard ramekins. 5. Pour water into the pot. Then place the bottom layer of the Deluxe Reversible Rack in the lower position in the pot. 6. Place the ramekins on the rack. Close the lid and move slider to PRESSURE. Ensuring the pressure release valve is in the SEAL position. The temperature will default to HIGH, which is the correct setting. Set time to 6 minutes. Select START/STOP to begin cooking. 7. When cooking is complete, naturally release the pressure for 10 minutes. Then release the pressure quickly by turning the pressure release valve to the VENT position. Move slider to AIR FRY/ STOVETOP to unlock the lid, then carefully open it. 8. Transfer custards to a plate and refrigerate covered for 2 hours. Serve.
Per Serving: Calories 294; Fat 15.96g; Sodium 204mg; Carbs 31.35g; Fibre 0.1g; Sugar 27.2g; Protein 6.83g

Carrot Coconut Cake with Pecans

Prep time: 10 minutes | **Cook time:** 20 minutes | **Serves:** 4

60 g coconut oil, melted
100 g sugar
1 large egg
½ teaspoon ground cinnamon
Pinch of ground nutmeg
½ teaspoon vanilla extract

30 g peeled, grated carrot
30 g unsweetened coconut flakes
60 g plain flour
½ teaspoon baking powder
30 g chopped pecans
240 ml water

1. Combine oil, sugar, egg, carrot, coconut flakes, cinnamon, vanilla, nutmeg, flour, and baking powder in a medium-sized bowl using a whisk. Be careful not to mix too much. 2. Add pecans by folding them in. Place the batter into a 15 cm cake pan that has been greased. 3. Pour water into the pot. Then place the bottom layer of the Deluxe Reversible Rack in the lower position in the pot. 4. Place the cake pan on the rack. Close the lid and move slider to PRESSURE. Ensuring the pressure release valve is in the SEAL position. The temperature will default to HIGH, which is the correct setting. Set time to 20 minutes. Select START/STOP to begin cooking. 5. When cooking is complete, naturally release the pressure for 5 minutes. Then release the pressure quickly by turning the pressure release valve to the VENT position. Move slider to AIR FRY/ STOVETOP to unlock the lid, then carefully open it. 6. Remove cake pan from the pot and transfer to a rack until cool. Flip cake onto a serving platter.
Per Serving: Calories 310; Fat 20.89g; Sodium 24mg; Carbs 29.46g; Fibre 1.9g; Sugar 14.9g; Protein 3.1g

Delicious Maple Crème Brule

Prep time: 20 minutes | **Cook time:** 15 minutes | **Serves:** 3

320 g heavy whipping cream
3 large egg yolks
105 g packed brown sugar
Topping:
1½ tsp. sugar

¼ tsp. ground cinnamon
½ tsp. maple flavouring
240 ml water

1½ tsp. brown sugar

1. Move slider to AIR FRY/STOVETOP. Select SEAR/SAUTÉ and set to Lo1. Select START/STOP to begin preheating. 2. Add cream. Heat until bubbles form around sides of cooker. Mix together egg yolks, brown sugar and cinnamon in a small bowl. Press START/STOP to turn off the SEAR/SAUTÉ function. 3. Stir a small amount of hot cream into egg mixture. Return all to the pressure cooker, stirring frequently. Stir in maple flavouring. 4. Transfer cream mixture to three greased. ramekins or custard cups. Wipe pressure cooker clean. Pour in water, then place the bottom layer of the Deluxe Reversible Rack in the lower position in the pot. 5. Place ramekins on the rack, loosely cover with foil to prevent moisture from getting into ramekins. 6. Close the lid and move slider to PRESSURE. Ensuring the pressure release valve is in the SEAL position. The temperature will default to HIGH, which is the correct setting. Set time to 10 minutes. Select START/STOP to begin cooking. 7. When cooking is complete, naturally release the pressure for 10 minutes. Then release the pressure quickly by turning the pressure release valve to the VENT position. Move slider to AIR FRY/ STOVETOP to unlock the lid, then carefully open it. 8. A knife inserted in the centre should come out clean, though centre will still be soft. Using tongs, remove ramekins. Cool for 10 minutes; refrigerate, covered, for at least 4 hours. 9. For the topping, combine sugars and sprinkle over ramekins. Hold a kitchen torch about 2 in. above custard surface; rotate slowly until sugar is evenly caramelized. Serve right away.

Per Serving: Calories 395; Fat 24.2g; Sodium 41mg; Carbs 42.51g; Fibre 0.1g; Sugar 41.29g; Protein 3.84g

Conclusion

A feature-rich kitchen gadget, the Ninja Foodi Max Multi Cooker may be used for air frying, steaming, pressure cooking, and more. The Ninja Foodi Max Multi-excellent cooker's cooking features and enormous capacity to feed the entire family make it quick and simple to prepare delectable dinners, sides, snacks, and desserts. An entire chicken may fit in and be cooked in the fryer basket, which has a good capacity. Utilize pressure cooking to cook delicate meals up to 70% quicker than conventional methods, followed by crisping to give your food a beautiful golden finish.

Appendix Recipes Index

A
Autumn Potatoes Egg Salad 51
B
Balsamic Mozzarella Chicken Veggie Salad 59
Banana-Nutella Stuffed French Toast 19
Banana-Walnuts Oatmeal 18
Barbecue Beef & Pasta Casserole 87
Beans and Kale Soup 30
Beef and Carrot Stew with Bacon 76
Beef and Mushroom Stroganoff Soup 39
Beef and Sausage Soup with Pepperoni 30
Beef Brisket & Butternut Squash Chili 35
Beef Lettuce Wraps 79
Beef Sandwiches with Cheese Sauce 78
Beef, Barley and Celery Soup 88
Beer-Braised Pork with Sauerkraut 85
Beer-Braised Pulled Beef 89
Best Key Lime Pie 96
Black Bean & Brown Rice Casserole 49
Black Bean and Rice–Stuffed Peppers 48
Black-Eyed Peas and Ham Soup 39
Breakfast Farro with Apricots 19
Buckwheat Banana Porridge 21
C
Cajun Chicken and Rice Bowls 53
Caramel Brownie Pudding 95
Carrot Coconut Cake with Pecans 98
Cheddar Broccoli and Potato Soup 31
Cheese and Courgette Stuffed Chicken 56
Cheese Broccoli Potato Cake 48
Cheese Pasta with Broccoli 43
Cheese Sausage and Egg Strata 18
Cheesecake with Peaches 92
Cheesy Alfredo Pasta with Carrots & Broccoli 49
Cheesy Broccoli, Carrot and Cauliflower Soup 40
Cheesy Spaghetti with Sausage and Broccolini 46
Cheesy Tortellini Alfredo and Peas 43

Chicken & Dumplings Soup 61
Chicken and Bacon Sandwiches 58
Chili Beef Hot Dog Soup 32
Chinese-Style Chicken & Broccoli 64
Chocolate Banana Bread 17
Chocolate-Berry Mug Cake 94
Classic Cheesecake 93
Coffee-Rubbed Steak and Rice Bowls 80
Corned Beef and Beans Chili 28
Cranberry & Walnuts Stuffed Apples 97
Cranberry Hot Chicken Wings 55
Creamy Cheese Chicken Soup 29
Creamy Cheese Tomato Basil Soup 32
Creamy Curry Chicken Bites 62
Creamy Polenta 20
Creamy Seafood and Noodles Casserole 70
Creamy Seafood Chowder 75
Creamy Strawberry Oats 26
Cumin Bacon and Black Bean Chili 36
Cumin Salsa Verde Chicken 58
Curried Prawns with Vegetables & Rice Vermicelli 70
D
Delicious Maple Crème Brule 99
Delicious Prawns Stew with White Beans & Spinach 68
Delicious Stuffed Peaches 93
E
Easy Beef and Broccoli 82
Easy White Chocolate Pots De Crème 98
F
French Onion Cheese Chicken 60
French Onion Cheese Soup 27
Fundamentals of Ninja Foodi Max Multi-Cooker 2
G
Garlic Cheese Bread 25
Garlicky Buttery Prawns 74
Garlicky Pork Roast with Red Cabbage 85
Garlicky Salmon 68

101 | Appendix Recipes Index

Greek Chicken and Mixed Greens Salad 52

H

Herbed Beef & Cheddar Croissants 81

Herbed Clams 71

Herbed Crab Cake 73

Herbed Kidney Bean and Sausage Soup 40

Homemade Beef & Beets Borscht 77

Homemade Gingerbread French Toast Casserole 26

Homemade Molten Mocha Cake 92

Honey Veggie Corn Muffins 22

I

Indian Curried Chicken 54

Indian-Spiced Basmati Rice with Peas 44

Israeli Couscous and Veggie 23

J

Jalapeno & Cotija Cheese Potato Pie 47

Jalapeño-Cheddar Bagel Egg Casserole 25

Jollof Rice With Prawns & Peas 67

Juicy Chicken Sliders 57

K

Kale and Edamame Salad with Sesame Ginger Dressing 46

Korean Beef Rolls 80

L

Lamb and Carrot Stew 38

Lemny Salmon with Horseradish Sauce 71

Lemony Beef Risotto 79

Lemony Chicken with Artichoke Avocado 56

Lemony Mushroom and Leeks Risotto 44

Lemony Tapioca Pudding 96

Lima Beans with Bacon & Tomato 45

Lime Prawns & Corn Salad 69

Loaded Vegetable and Green Lentil Stew 37

M

Marsala Wine Braised Chicken and Mushroom 63

Mushroom Congee Breakfast Bowl 24

Mustard Potato and Bacon Salad 45

P

Peach-Berry Cobbler 94

Pearled Barley-Lentil Soup with Spinach 33

Pepperoni, Cheese Ravioli and Mushroom Pizza Stew 34

Pork Chops with Creamy Mushroom Gravy 87

Prawns and Potatoes with Cocktail Sauce 74

Pulled Beef with Pappardelle 83

Pulled Lamb Shoulder with Pomegranate & Honey Sauce 86

Pulled Pork and Pineapple Sandwiches 78

Q

Quinoa Chili with Feta cheese 21

R

Red Wine-Braised Apples 95

Red Wine–Braised Beef Short Ribs 84

Rice Pilaf withCorn and Prawns 66

Rosemary Apricot Scones 24

Rosemary Navy Beans 50

S

Salmon, Leek, and Potato Soup 28

Seafood and Veggie Stew 72

Simple Corn on the Cob (Four Ways) 41

Smoked Paprika Turkey Lunchmeat 57

Spanish Rice with Pepper s 42

Spiced Corn with Jalapeno-Peppers 47

Spiced Mango-Chipotle Shredded Chicken 59

Spiced Red Lentil and Pumpkin Soup 37

Spiced Yellow Lentil and Spinach Soup 31

Spicy Black Bean Soup 33

Spicy Pork Chorizo with Mexican Eggs 22

Steel-Cut Oats with Dried Apples 20

Sweet Potato Lentil Soup with Spinach 38

T

Tasty Barbecue Chicken–Stuffed Sweet Potatoes 54

Tasty Courgette & Cheese Drop Biscuits 23

Tasty Pickled Pulled Pork 88

Teriyaki Chicken Wings 53

Teriyaki Pulled Lamb 90

Thai Spiced Lentil and Coconut Milk Soup 34

Thai-Style Butternut Bisque 29

Turkey Meatball and Kale Soup with White Beans 65

Turkey Verde and Brown Rice 55

V

Vanilla Cheesecake 91

Vanilla Lemon Cheesecake 97

Vegetarian Gumbo with Rice 50

W

White Rice with Peas and Swiss Chard 42

Y

Yellow Lentil Soup 36